QUEENSLAND

TRAVEL GUIDE 2023

Thrilling Tropical Adventures: Explore Queensland's lush landscapes for unforgettable experiences.

Robben Charles

DISCLAIMER

The Queensland Travel Guide 2023 by Robben Charles provides general information and recommendations, but we cannot guarantee its absolute accuracy or timeliness. Readers are responsible for verifying details with official sources. We do not assume liability for any loss or inconvenience incurred while relying on this guide. External links and personal preferences are beyond our control. Travelers should comply with laws and exercise discretion. By using this guide, readers accept that we are not liable for any issues arising from its use. Consult authorities and conduct personal research for a safe and enjoyable trip to Queensland.

TABLE OF CONTENTS

Table of Contents

Welcome to Queensland

Introduction

Welcome to Queensland

Welcome to Queensland, Australia's beautiful Sunshine State! Located in the northeastern part of the country, Queensland is renowned for its stunning coastline, tropical rainforests, vibrant cities, and unique wildlife. Whether you're an adventure seeker, nature lover, beach bum, or culture enthusiast, Queensland offers a wide range of experiences that will leave you captivated and eager to explore more.

Geography:
Spanning over 1.8 million square kilometers, Queensland is Australia's second-largest state. It shares borders with the Northern Territory, South Australia, and New South Wales. The state's diverse landscape includes

the iconic Great Barrier Reef, the world's largest coral reef system, stretching over 2,300 kilometers along the coast. Queensland also boasts the breathtaking Wet Tropics Rainforest, a UNESCO World Heritage site, as well as vast outback regions and picturesque mountain ranges.

Cities and Regions:
Queensland is home to vibrant cities and charming towns that cater to different interests. The capital city, Brisbane, is a cosmopolitan hub with a thriving arts scene, bustling markets, and a vibrant riverfront. Along the coast, you'll find the popular holiday destinations of Gold Coast and Sunshine Coast, known for their pristine beaches, thrilling theme parks, and surfing spots. Cairns, located in the Tropical North Queensland region, serves as the gateway to the Great Barrier Reef and is a popular base for exploring the Daintree Rainforest.

Natural Wonders:
Queensland's natural wonders are awe-inspiring and offer a myriad of outdoor activities. The Great Barrier Reef is a diver's paradise, with vibrant coral formations and a kaleidoscope of marine life. The Whitsunday Islands, situated in the heart of the reef, feature secluded beaches and crystal-clear waters, perfect for snorkeling, sailing, or simply relaxing. Further inland, you'll discover the ancient beauty of the Daintree Rainforest, where lush vegetation, exotic wildlife, and tranquil waterfalls await.

Adventure and Wildlife:
Adventure seekers will find plenty to do in Queensland. The state offers thrilling experiences such as bungee jumping, skydiving, and white-water rafting. For wildlife enthusiasts, Queensland is a treasure trove. You can witness the annual turtle

nesting at Mon Repos near Bundaberg, get up close with koalas on Magnetic Island, or spot humpback whales along the coastline during their annual migration. The Australia Zoo, founded by the late conservationist Steve Irwin, is also a must-visit attraction.

Indigenous Culture:
Queensland is home to a rich Indigenous heritage, with numerous Aboriginal and Torres Strait Islander communities preserving their traditions and sharing their stories. Visitors can immerse themselves in Indigenous culture through art exhibitions, guided tours, and cultural performances. The Tjapukai Aboriginal Cultural Park near Cairns and the Jagera Aboriginal Cultural Center in Brisbane offer insightful experiences into the local Indigenous cultures.

Events and Festivals:

Queensland hosts a vibrant calendar of events and festivals throughout the year. The Brisbane Festival, held annually in September, showcases a range of artistic performances, music, and cultural exhibitions. The Gold Coast hosts the popular Surfers Paradise Festival, featuring live entertainment, food stalls, and beachside activities. The Cairns Indigenous Art Fair celebrates the diverse arts and crafts of Aboriginal and Torres Strait Islander artists.

Queensland truly offers something for everyone, from its stunning natural landscapes and thrilling adventures to its rich cultural heritage and welcoming communities. So, get ready to explore this remarkable state and create memories that will last a lifetime. Welcome to Queensland, where adventure and relaxation await at every turn!

About this Guide

Welcome to this comprehensive guide to Queensland, Australia's captivating Sunshine State! Whether you're planning a trip to Queensland or simply seeking to learn more about this fascinating region, this guide aims to provide you with all the essential information and insights you need to make the most of your experience.

1. **Discovering Queensland:** This section offers an overview of Queensland's geography, highlighting its vast size, diverse landscapes, and iconic natural wonders. Learn about the state's breathtaking coastline, tropical rainforests, outback regions, and mountain ranges that make it a haven for outdoor enthusiasts and nature lovers.

2. **Exploring Cities and Regions:** Queensland is home to a range of vibrant cities and charming towns, each with its own unique

character and attractions. In this section, we'll delve into the major cities such as Brisbane, the capital city, known for its cultural offerings and vibrant urban lifestyle. We'll also explore popular coastal destinations like the Gold Coast and Sunshine Coast, as well as tropical hotspots like Cairns and the Whitsunday Islands.

3. **Must-See Attractions:** Queensland is brimming with must-see attractions that showcase the state's natural beauty and cultural heritage. From the world-famous Great Barrier Reef and its remarkable marine life to the ancient wonders of the Daintree Rainforest, this section highlights the top attractions that make Queensland a dream destination for travelers.

4. **Outdoor Adventures:** If you're seeking adventure and adrenaline-pumping experiences, Queensland won't disappoint.

Discover a range of thrilling outdoor activities such as diving and snorkeling in the Great Barrier Reef, exploring the rugged landscapes of the Outback, chasing waterfalls in national parks, or embarking on exhilarating wildlife encounters.

5. **Indigenous Culture:** Queensland has a rich Indigenous heritage, and this section explores the vibrant cultures of Aboriginal and Torres Strait Islander communities. Learn about the art, traditions, and cultural experiences available, including guided tours, art exhibitions, and festivals that celebrate and honor Indigenous culture.

6. **Festivals and Events:** Queensland hosts a variety of exciting festivals and events throughout the year. From music festivals and cultural celebrations to sporting events and agricultural shows, this section highlights the top happenings in the state, allowing you to

plan your visit around these vibrant experiences.

7. **Practical Information:** Planning a trip requires practical information, and this section covers everything you need to know about transportation, accommodation options, weather patterns, local cuisine, and essential travel tips. It aims to ensure that you have a smooth and enjoyable journey throughout Queensland.

8. **Insider Tips:** To enhance your experience and make the most of your time in Queensland, this section provides insider tips and recommendations from locals and experienced travelers. Discover hidden gems, off-the-beaten-path destinations, and insider knowledge that will help you create unforgettable memories.

Whether you're drawn to Queensland's natural wonders, seeking adventure, or interested in immersing yourself in its vibrant culture, this guide will serve as your companion, providing you with the knowledge and inspiration to embark on an extraordinary journey through Queensland, the Sunshine State of Australia.

Essential Information

Before embarking on your journey to Queensland, it's important to familiarize yourself with some essential information to ensure a smooth and enjoyable experience. Here are the key details you need to know:

1. **Location and Geography:** Queensland is located in the northeastern part of Australia. It shares borders with the Northern Territory, South Australia, and New South Wales. The state covers a vast area of over 1.8 million square kilometers, offering diverse landscapes ranging from stunning coastlines and tropical rainforests to outback regions and mountain ranges.

2. **Climate**: Queensland experiences a range of climates due to its vast size. In general, the state has a tropical and subtropical climate, with warm to hot temperatures year-round. Coastal areas enjoy a pleasant climate, while

inland regions can experience hotter and drier conditions. It's advisable to check the weather patterns and pack accordingly for your specific destinations and activities.

3. **Best Time to Visit:** Queensland is a year-round destination, but the best time to visit may vary depending on your preferences and activities. The coastal regions are popular during the summer months (December to February) when you can enjoy beach activities and water sports. The winter months (June to August) offer milder temperatures and are ideal for exploring the outdoors and wildlife encounters. It's recommended to research the specific regions you plan to visit and consider the weather, peak tourist seasons, and any events or festivals happening during your preferred travel period.

4. **Getting There:** Queensland is well-connected domestically and

internationally. Brisbane Airport is the major gateway, with numerous flights from major cities in Australia and direct flights from various international destinations. Other regional airports, such as Cairns and Gold Coast airports, also have regular domestic and international flights. If traveling within Australia, you can also consider road trips or train journeys to reach Queensland.

5. **Visa Requirements:** International visitors to Australia generally require a visa, unless they come from visa-exempt countries. It's essential to check the visa requirements specific to your nationality and duration of stay. The most common visa for tourists is the Visitor Visa (subclass 600), which allows for leisure travel and stays of up to three months. Ensure that your passport has at least six months of validity beyond your planned departure date.

6. **Currency**: The currency in Australia is the Australian Dollar (AUD). ATMs are widely available in cities and towns, and credit cards are accepted in most establishments. It's advisable to inform your bank or credit card company about your travel plans to avoid any issues with card usage.

7. **Transportation**: Queensland has a well-developed transportation network, making it easy to explore the state. In major cities like Brisbane, you'll find public transportation options such as buses, trains, and ferries. Renting a car is a popular choice for exploring regional areas and the coast. Additionally, there are domestic flights, coach services, and scenic train routes available for longer journeys within Queensland.

8. **Safety and Health**: Queensland is generally a safe destination for travelers. It's recommended to take normal precautions,

such as keeping an eye on your belongings, using reputable transportation services, and being aware of your surroundings. As with any travel, it's advisable to have travel insurance that covers medical expenses and any specific activities you plan to undertake. Queensland has a reliable healthcare system, and major cities have hospitals and medical facilities.

9. **Time Zone:** Queensland operates on Australian Eastern Standard Time (AEST), which is 10 hours ahead of Coordinated Universal Time (UTC+10). However, Queensland does not observe daylight saving time, except for certain regions like the Southern Gold Coast.

10. **Important Contacts**: It's useful to have important contact information readily available during your stay. The emergency number in Australia is 000 for immediate assistance in case of emergencies.

Getting to Queensland

By Air

Getting to Queensland by air is a convenient and efficient option for travelers from both domestic and international locations. Queensland is home to several major airports, offering excellent connectivity and a wide range of flight options. Here is some detailed information about getting to Queensland by air:

International Airports:

1. Brisbane Airport (BNE): Located in Brisbane, the state capital of Queensland, Brisbane Airport is the primary international gateway to the state. It serves as a major hub for both domestic and international flights, offering connections to various destinations worldwide. Airlines such as Qantas, Virgin

Australia, and international carriers operate regular flights to and from Brisbane Airport.

Domestic Airports:
1. Cairns Airport (CNS): Situated in Cairns, a popular tourist destination in North Queensland, Cairns Airport serves as a major domestic hub for the region. It offers direct flights to and from major Australian cities, including Sydney, Melbourne, Brisbane, and Perth. Cairns Airport is also the primary gateway to the Great Barrier Reef.

2. Gold Coast Airport (OOL): Located near Coolangatta, the Gold Coast Airport is a popular entry point for travelers visiting the Gold Coast region and its surrounding areas. It offers a range of domestic flights, connecting to cities like Sydney, Melbourne, Adelaide, and Hobart. Some international flights also operate from Gold Coast Airport, providing

connections to destinations such as New Zealand and Southeast Asia.

3. Townsville Airport (TSV): Situated in Townsville, a city in North Queensland, Townsville Airport serves as an important regional airport. It offers domestic flights to major Australian cities, including Brisbane, Sydney, and Melbourne. The airport is a convenient entry point for visitors exploring the Great Barrier Reef, Magnetic Island, and other nearby attractions.

4. Sunshine Coast Airport (MCY): Located near Maroochydore, the Sunshine Coast Airport serves as the main airport for travelers visiting the Sunshine Coast region. It provides domestic flights to cities like Sydney, Melbourne, Adelaide, and Auckland (New Zealand). The airport offers easy access to popular destinations such as Noosa, Mooloolaba, and the Hinterland.

Flight Options:

Numerous airlines operate flights to Queensland, catering to both domestic and international travelers. Some major airlines include Qantas, Virgin Australia, Jetstar Airways, Air New Zealand, Singapore Airlines, Emirates, and Cathay Pacific. These airlines provide a range of options in terms of flight times, fares, and service classes, ensuring flexibility for travelers.

Airport Transfers and Ground Transportation: Upon arrival at the airports, various transportation options are available to reach your desired destination within Queensland. These include:

1. **Taxis and Rideshare:** Taxis and rideshare services such as Uber are readily available at the airports, offering convenient

transportation to your accommodation or other destinations.

2. **Airport Shuttles**: Many airports provide shuttle services, which are often pre-booked and offer shared or private transfers to popular destinations within the region. These shuttles can be a cost-effective and hassle-free option.

3. **Car Rentals**: Multiple car rental companies have counters at the airports, allowing travelers to hire vehicles and explore Queensland at their own pace. It is advisable to book in advance to secure the preferred vehicle.

4. **Public Transportation**: Public buses, trains, and trams are available in some airport locations, offering affordable transportation options to various destinations. It is

recommended to check the local transport authority's website for schedules and routes.

Traveling to Queensland by air provides easy access to the state's diverse attractions, stunning coastline, vibrant cities, and natural wonders. With well-connected airports and a wide range of flight options, visitors can enjoy a seamless and comfortable journey to this beautiful part of Australia.

By Land

Getting to Queensland by land offers travelers an alternative way to reach this vibrant Australian state. Whether you prefer the flexibility of driving or the convenience of bus and train services, here are some details and information on getting to Queensland by land:

1. **Driving**:
Queensland is well connected by an extensive road network, making it accessible from various locations within Australia. The major highways leading to Queensland include:

- Pacific Motorway (M1): Connects Queensland with New South Wales and extends from Sydney to Brisbane. It is the main road route for travelers driving between Sydney and Brisbane.

- Bruce Highway (A1): Stretches along the eastern coast of Queensland, connecting major cities such as Brisbane, Sunshine Coast, and Cairns. It provides access to popular destinations including the Great Barrier Reef, Fraser Island, and the Whitsunday Islands.

- New England Highway (A15): Runs from New South Wales through the Darling Downs region of Queensland, connecting with the Bruce Highway in Toowoomba.

- Warrego Highway (A2): Links Brisbane with Toowoomba and further west into the Darling Downs region of Queensland.

- Carnarvon Highway (A7): Connects St. George in Queensland to Injune, providing access to the stunning Carnarvon Gorge.

When planning a road trip to Queensland, it is essential to consider the distance, road conditions, and weather conditions, especially if traveling during the rainy season or in remote areas. Take note of rest stops, petrol stations, and accommodations along the way for a comfortable journey.

2. **Bus Services**:
Several bus companies operate services to Queensland, offering an affordable and convenient mode of transportation. Greyhound Australia is a prominent long-distance bus operator, providing connections between major Australian cities and regional towns in Queensland. Their extensive network covers destinations such as Brisbane, Cairns, Gold Coast, Sunshine Coast, and Townsville.

3. **Train Services:**
Queensland Rail operates train services within Queensland and offers scenic journeys for those who prefer a relaxed and picturesque travel experience. The two main long-distance train services are:

- The Spirit of Queensland: A modern and comfortable train that runs between Brisbane and Cairns. It provides panoramic views of Queensland's diverse landscapes, including coastal vistas and lush rainforests.

- The Spirit of the Outback: This train service connects Brisbane with Longreach, taking passengers through the vast and captivating Outback region of Queensland.

Queensland Rail also operates shorter regional services, such as the Tilt Train and the Sunlander, which offer travel between various destinations within the state.

4. Border Crossings:
If you are traveling to Queensland from another Australian state, it's important to check the border crossing requirements, especially during times when border

restrictions may be in place. Each state and territory in Australia may have different entry requirements and travel restrictions, so it's advisable to visit the official government websites for the latest information.

Whether you choose to drive, take a bus, or enjoy a scenic train journey, traveling to Queensland by land offers the opportunity to explore the state's diverse landscapes, charming towns, and iconic attractions at your own pace.

By Sea

Getting to Queensland by sea is an exciting and unique way to reach this beautiful Australian state. Queensland boasts several ports that accommodate cruise ships, ferries, and private vessels. Here are details and information on getting to Queensland by sea:

1. **Cruise Ships:**
Queensland is a popular cruise destination, attracting numerous cruise lines that offer voyages to various parts of the state. Major cruise ports in Queensland include:

- Port of Brisbane: Located in Brisbane, the state capital, the Port of Brisbane is a bustling cruise terminal that serves as a gateway for both domestic and international cruise ships. It offers a range of cruise itineraries, including trips to the Great Barrier Reef, the Whitsunday Islands, and other coastal destinations.

- Port of Cairns: Situated in Cairns, a city in North Queensland, the Port of Cairns is a significant cruise port, particularly for ships visiting the Great Barrier Reef and the tropical rainforests of the region. It provides access to iconic destinations like the Daintree Rainforest and the Coral Sea.

- Port of Townsville: Located in Townsville, the Port of Townsville is another entry point for cruise ships visiting North Queensland. It offers opportunities for exploring Magnetic Island, the Great Barrier Reef, and other attractions in the area.

Cruise ships typically offer a variety of amenities and activities on board, allowing passengers to enjoy the journey while visiting multiple destinations along the Queensland coast.

2. Ferries and Island Transfers:

Queensland is renowned for its stunning islands, and several ferry services provide transportation to these picturesque destinations. Some notable ferry routes include:

- Brisbane to Moreton Island: Regular ferry services operate from Brisbane to Moreton Island, offering passengers the chance to explore this idyllic island with its pristine beaches, sand dunes, and marine life.

- Airlie Beach to Whitsunday Islands: Airlie Beach serves as the gateway to the Whitsunday Islands, and ferries and island transfers depart from here, providing access to iconic locations such as Hamilton Island, Daydream Island, and Whitehaven Beach.

- Cairns to Fitzroy Island and Green Island: From Cairns, visitors can take ferries to

Fitzroy Island and Green Island, both known for their crystal-clear waters, coral reefs, and lush vegetation.

3. **Private Vessels**:
Travelers with private boats or yachts have the option to sail to Queensland and explore its coastal areas and islands at their leisure. Several marinas and ports along the Queensland coastline provide facilities for docking and mooring private vessels. It's essential to check with local authorities and marina operators for information on permits, docking fees, and any specific regulations or navigation requirements.

4. **Coastal Shipping Services**:
Queensland also has a few coastal shipping services that transport cargo and passengers along the coast. While these services may not be as common or frequent as other transportation options, they offer a unique

and off-the-beaten-path experience for travelers looking to explore Queensland's more remote regions.

When planning a journey to Queensland by sea, it's important to consider factors such as cruise itineraries, ferry schedules, and any required reservations or permits. Additionally, it's advisable to check the latest travel advisories, weather conditions, and any entry requirements or protocols in place. Whether embarking on a cruise, taking a ferry, or sailing on a private vessel, traveling to Queensland by sea allows you to experience the coastal beauty and island wonders of this captivating state.

Queensland Regions

Brisbane

Brisbane is the capital city of the Australian state of Queensland. It is the largest city in Queensland and the third-largest city in Australia, with a population of over 2.5 million people. Brisbane is situated on the eastern coast of Australia, along the banks of the Brisbane River, and enjoys a subtropical climate with warm summers and mild winters.

Here are some key details and information about Brisbane:

1. **Geography and Location**:
   - Brisbane is located in the southeastern corner of Queensland, on the east coast of Australia.

- The city is situated between Moreton Bay to the east and the Great Dividing Range to the west.

- It covers an area of approximately 15,842 square kilometers (6,118 square miles).

2. **History**:

- The area where Brisbane is located has been inhabited by Indigenous Australians for thousands of years.

- European settlement in the area began in 1824 when a penal colony was established at Redcliffe, about 28 kilometers (17 miles) north of present-day Brisbane.

- The colony was later moved to its current location along the Brisbane River in 1825 and named after Sir Thomas Brisbane, the Governor of New South Wales at the time.

3. **Economy**:

- Brisbane is a major economic hub in Australia, with diverse industries driving its economy.
- Key sectors include finance, education, information technology, tourism, manufacturing, and health services.
- The city is home to numerous multinational companies and has a thriving entrepreneurial and startup ecosystem.

4. **Landmarks and Attractions**:
- South Bank Parklands: A popular recreational area along the southern bank of the Brisbane River, featuring parklands, gardens, swimming pools, and a man-made beach.
- Brisbane City Botanic Gardens: Located in the heart of the city, these gardens showcase a wide variety of tropical and subtropical plants.
- Queensland Cultural Centre: A precinct in South Bank that houses the Queensland Museum, Queensland Art Gallery, Gallery of

Modern Art (GOMA), and the State Library of Queensland.

- Story Bridge: An iconic bridge that spans the Brisbane River and offers panoramic views of the city skyline.

- Lone Pine Koala Sanctuary: The world's oldest and largest koala sanctuary, located in the suburb of Fig Tree Pocket.

5. **Education**:

- Brisbane is home to several universities, including the University of Queensland (UQ), Queensland University of Technology (QUT), and Griffith University.

- These universities are renowned for their research and offer a wide range of academic programs.

6. **Transportation**:

- Brisbane has an extensive public transportation network, including buses, trains, and ferries, operated by TransLink.

- Brisbane Airport, located approximately 17 kilometers (10.5 miles) northeast of the city center, is the primary gateway to the region and offers domestic and international flights.

7. **Events and Festivals:**
  - Brisbane hosts numerous events and festivals throughout the year, including the Brisbane Festival, Riverfire, and the Brisbane Ekka (Royal Queensland Show).
  - The city is known for its vibrant arts and cultural scene, with theaters, galleries, and live music venues.

Brisbane offers a combination of natural beauty, cultural attractions, and a vibrant city lifestyle, making it a popular destination for residents and visitors alike.

Gold Coast

The Gold Coast is a region located in the southeastern part of the Australian state of Queensland. It is renowned for its beautiful beaches, vibrant entertainment, and tourism industry. Here are some details and information about the Gold Coast region:

1. Geography and Location:

- The Gold Coast is situated on the eastern coast of Australia, about 66 kilometers (41 miles) south of the state capital, Brisbane.

- It stretches along the coastline for approximately 57 kilometers (35 miles), bordered by the Pacific Ocean to the east and the hinterland to the west.

- The region covers an area of around 1,334 square kilometers (515 square miles).

2. Cities and Local Government Areas:

- The Gold Coast region includes several cities and local government areas, including the City of Gold Coast, which is the largest local government area in Australia by population.

   - Other notable cities and areas within the region include Surfers Paradise, Broadbeach, Burleigh Heads, Coolangatta, and Southport.

3. **Tourism and Attractions**:
   - The Gold Coast is a major tourist destination known for its stunning sandy beaches, surfing spots, and high-rise buildings.
   - Surfers Paradise, located in the heart of the region, is a popular entertainment hub with a vibrant nightlife, shopping precincts, and dining options.
   - The theme parks in the area, such as Dreamworld, Sea World, Warner Bros. Movie World, and Wet'n'Wild, attract millions of visitors each year.
   - The Gold Coast Hinterland, with its lush rainforests, waterfalls, and national parks,

offers a peaceful retreat from the coastal bustle and provides opportunities for hiking, camping, and exploring nature.

4. **Economy**:

  - The Gold Coast has a diverse economy with tourism being one of its major industries.

  - The region attracts domestic and international visitors, contributing significantly to the local economy through accommodation, hospitality, entertainment, and retail sectors.

  - Other key sectors include education, health services, construction, film production, and information technology.

5. **Sports and Events**:

  - The Gold Coast has a strong sporting culture and has hosted major events such as the Commonwealth Games in 2018.

  - It is home to several professional sporting teams, including the Gold Coast Suns

(Australian Rules Football) and the Gold Coast Titans (Rugby League).

- The region also hosts various sporting events, including the Gold Coast Marathon, Gold Coast 600 (V8 Supercars), and Quiksilver Pro Gold Coast (surfing).

6. Education:

- The Gold Coast is home to several universities and educational institutions, including Griffith University and Bond University.
- These institutions offer a wide range of academic programs and contribute to the region's reputation as an educational hub.

7. Transportation:

- The Gold Coast is well-connected by road, with the Pacific Motorway (M1) providing easy access to Brisbane and other parts of Queensland.

- Gold Coast Airport, located in Coolangatta, offers domestic and international flights, connecting the region to various destinations.

The Gold Coast region offers a unique blend of natural beauty, entertainment, and recreational opportunities, making it a popular destination for tourists, students, and residents seeking a coastal lifestyle with abundant amenities.

Sunshine Coast

The Sunshine Coast is a picturesque region located in the southeastern part of the Australian state of Queensland. It is renowned for its stunning coastline, pristine beaches, lush hinterland, and relaxed coastal lifestyle. Here are some details and information about the Sunshine Coast region:

1. **Geography and Location:**
   - The Sunshine Coast is situated on the eastern coast of Australia, about 100 kilometers (62 miles) north of the state capital, Brisbane.
   - It spans approximately 65 kilometers (40 miles) of coastline along the Pacific Ocean, extending from Caloundra in the south to Rainbow Beach in the north.
   - The region covers an area of around 2,227 square kilometers (860 square miles).

2. **Cities and Local Government Areas:**

- The Sunshine Coast region includes several cities, towns, and local government areas, including the major urban centers of Maroochydore, Mooloolaba, Caloundra, and Noosa.

- Other notable areas within the region include Coolum, Nambour, Maleny, Montville, and Eumundi.

3. Beaches and Natural Beauty:

- The Sunshine Coast is known for its pristine sandy beaches, crystal-clear waters, and ideal surfing conditions.

- Popular beaches in the region include Mooloolaba Beach, Noosa Main Beach, Coolum Beach, and Kings Beach.

- The Sunshine Coast hinterland offers breathtaking scenery with lush rainforests, cascading waterfalls, and panoramic views from the Glass House Mountains.

4. Tourism and Attractions:

- The Sunshine Coast is a major tourist destination, attracting visitors with its natural beauty, outdoor activities, and family-friendly attractions.
- Noosa National Park, located on the eastern edge of the region, is renowned for its coastal trails, wildlife, and secluded beaches.
- Australia Zoo, founded by the late Steve Irwin, is a popular wildlife conservation park that showcases native Australian animals.
- The Eumundi Markets, held on Wednesdays and Saturdays, are famous for their arts, crafts, and local produce.

5. **Lifestyle and Culture:**
- The Sunshine Coast offers a relaxed coastal lifestyle, with a strong emphasis on outdoor activities, health, and well-being.
- The region is home to numerous surf schools, golf courses, cycling and walking trails, and water sports facilities.

- It has a vibrant arts and cultural scene, with galleries, theaters, music festivals, and a strong sense of community.

6. **Economy**:
  - The Sunshine Coast has a diverse economy with industries such as tourism, retail, construction, health services, education, and agribusiness.
  - The region is experiencing significant growth, attracting investment and fostering entrepreneurship in sectors such as technology and innovation.

7. **Education**:
  - The Sunshine Coast is home to the University of the Sunshine Coast (USC), which offers a range of undergraduate and postgraduate programs.
  - It also has several reputable primary and secondary schools, both public and private.

8. **Transportation**:

- The Sunshine Coast is well-connected by road, with the Bruce Highway providing access to Brisbane and other parts of Queensland.

- Sunshine Coast Airport, located in Marcoola, offers domestic and limited international flights, connecting the region to various destinations.

The Sunshine Coast region offers a relaxed coastal lifestyle, stunning natural beauty, and a range of recreational activities, making it a sought-after destination for tourists, retirees, and families seeking a laid-back and picturesque coastal living experience.

Tropical North Queensland

Tropical North Queensland is a captivating region located in the northern part of the Australian state of Queensland. It is renowned for its breathtaking natural landscapes, tropical rainforests, stunning coral reefs, and diverse wildlife. Here are some details and information about Tropical North Queensland:

1. Geography and Location:
   - Tropical North Queensland stretches along the northeastern coast of Queensland, from the city of Cairns in the south to the town of Cooktown in the north.
   - The region encompasses a vast area, covering approximately 78,000 square kilometers (30,116 square miles).
   - It is bordered by the Coral Sea to the east and the Great Dividing Range to the west.

2. Climate and Biodiversity:

- As the name suggests, Tropical North Queensland experiences a warm tropical climate with high humidity and distinct wet and dry seasons.
- The region is known for its rich biodiversity, housing numerous World Heritage-listed areas, including the Great Barrier Reef, Daintree Rainforest, and Wet Tropics of Queensland.
- The Great Barrier Reef, the world's largest coral reef system, stretches along the coast and offers unparalleled opportunities for snorkeling, scuba diving, and marine exploration.

3. **Cities and Towns:**
- The major city in the region is Cairns, which serves as the main gateway to Tropical North Queensland and is a popular tourist destination.

- Other notable towns and areas include Port Douglas, Palm Cove, Mission Beach, Cape Tribulation, and Cooktown.

- These towns offer a range of accommodation, dining, and entertainment options, as well as access to the region's natural attractions.

4. Natural Attractions:

- The Great Barrier Reef: This iconic natural wonder is a must-visit attraction, offering opportunities for snorkeling, diving, and boat tours to explore the vibrant coral reefs and marine life.

- Daintree Rainforest: As one of the oldest rainforests in the world, the Daintree is a UNESCO World Heritage site and home to unique flora and fauna, including the endangered cassowary.

- Atherton Tablelands: Located on the western part of the region, the Atherton Tablelands offer picturesque landscapes, waterfalls, lakes, and opportunities for wildlife spotting and hiking.

   - Mossman Gorge: Situated in the southern part of the Daintree Rainforest, Mossman Gorge is a popular destination for its crystal-clear waters, lush greenery, and Indigenous cultural experiences.

5. **Adventure and Outdoor Activities:**
   - Tropical North Queensland provides ample opportunities for adventure and outdoor activities.
   - Visitors can go snorkeling, diving, or take scenic helicopter rides to explore the Great Barrier Reef.
   - Rainforest walks, canopy tours, and river cruises offer opportunities to immerse in the natural beauty of the region.
   - White-water rafting, bungee jumping, and skydiving are popular adrenaline-pumping activities available in the area.

6. **Indigenous Culture:**

- Tropical North Queensland is rich in Indigenous culture, with a significant presence of Aboriginal and Torres Strait Islander communities.

- Visitors can engage in cultural experiences, such as guided tours, traditional performances, and learning about the ancient traditions and history of the local Indigenous peoples.

7. **Transportation:**

- Cairns International Airport serves as the main entry point for visitors to Tropical North Queensland, with domestic and international flights connecting the region to various destinations.

- The region is well-connected by road, and driving is a popular way to explore the area, with scenic coastal drives and inland routes.

Tropical North Queensland offers a unique blend of natural wonders, adventure, Indigenous culture, and a laid-back tropical atmosphere, making it a popular destination for nature enthusiasts, adventure seekers, and those looking to experience the wonders

Whitsundays

The Whitsundays is a stunning region located in the central part of the Australian state of Queensland. It is renowned for its pristine white-sand beaches, crystal-clear turquoise waters, and picturesque islands. Here are some details and information about the Whitsundays:

1. **Geography and Location**:
   - The Whitsundays is located on the central coast of Queensland, approximately 900 kilometers (560 miles) north of Brisbane.
   - The region encompasses a group of 74 islands, of which only a few are inhabited, including Hamilton Island, Daydream Island, and Whitsunday Island.
   - The mainland coastal towns of Airlie Beach and Bowen also form part of the Whitsundays region.

2. **The Great Barrier Reef:**

- The Whitsundays is nestled within the Great Barrier Reef, the world's largest coral reef system.

- The reef provides unparalleled opportunities for snorkeling, scuba diving, and boat tours to explore the vibrant coral gardens, diverse marine life, and underwater ecosystems.

- Heart Reef, a heart-shaped coral formation, is a famous attraction within the Great Barrier Reef and is often visited by scenic flights.

3. **Islands and Beaches:**

- The Whitsundays are famous for their breathtaking islands and beaches, with white silica sands and crystal-clear waters.

- Whitehaven Beach, located on Whitsunday Island, is an iconic stretch of beach known for its pure white sand and azure waters.

- Other popular island destinations include Hamilton Island, known for its luxurious resorts and marina, and Daydream Island, which offers family-friendly activities and beautiful coral reefs.

4. **Sailing and Boating:**

- The Whitsundays is a premier sailing destination, attracting sailing enthusiasts from around the world.

- Visitors can hire yachts, catamarans, or join organized sailing tours to explore the islands, anchor in secluded bays, and enjoy the tranquility of the marine playground.

5. **Wildlife and Nature:**

- The Whitsundays is home to a diverse range of wildlife, both on land and in the waters.

- Visitors may encounter dolphins, sea turtles, and humpback whales (during migration season) while exploring the region's waters.

- The islands and national parks within the Whitsundays offer opportunities for bushwalking, wildlife spotting, and birdwatching, with native species such as wallabies, possums, and a variety of birdlife.

6. **Great Walks and Lookouts**:

- The Ngaro Sea Trail and Whitsunday Great Walk offer stunning hiking experiences, allowing visitors to explore the lush rainforests, rugged coastal landscapes, and panoramic lookout points.

- Hill Inlet, a famous lookout on Whitsunday Island, provides breathtaking views of swirling sands and stunning shades of blue water.

7. **Access and Accommodation**:

- The Whitsundays can be accessed by flying into the Great Barrier Reef Airport on Hamilton Island or the Whitsunday Coast Airport near Proserpine.

- Airlie Beach serves as the main gateway to the Whitsunday Islands, offering a range of accommodation options, including resorts, hotels, and backpacker hostels.

The Whitsundays region offers a tropical paradise with its pristine beaches, idyllic islands, and the wonders of the Great Barrier Reef. It is a popular destination for sailing, snorkeling, and enjoying the natural beauty of one of Australia's most stunning coastal areas.

Great Barrier Reef

The Great Barrier Reef is a world-renowned natural wonder and one of the most iconic regions in the Australian state of Queensland. It is a vast and diverse ecosystem that stretches over 2,300 kilometers (1,400 miles) along the northeastern coast. Here are some details and information about the Great Barrier Reef:

1. **Location and Geography:**
   - The Great Barrier Reef is located off the coast of Queensland, parallel to the mainland.
   - It encompasses an area of approximately 344,400 square kilometers (133,000 square miles), making it the world's largest coral reef system.
   - The reef is composed of thousands of individual coral reefs, islands, and coral cays, creating a complex and interconnected ecosystem.

2. **Biodiversity and Marine Life:**

   - The Great Barrier Reef is renowned for its exceptional biodiversity, housing a wide range of marine species.

   - It is home to more than 1,500 species of fish, 600 types of coral, 3,000 varieties of mollusks, and numerous other marine organisms.

   - The reef provides habitats for endangered species, including green sea turtles, dugongs, and several species of whales.

3. **Coral Reefs and Marine Gardens:**

   - The Great Barrier Reef boasts stunning coral reefs and marine gardens, with intricate and vibrant underwater ecosystems.

   - The reefs are made up of hard and soft corals, forming a kaleidoscope of colors and shapes.

   - Snorkeling and scuba diving are popular activities for visitors to explore the reef's beauty, witnessing its diverse marine life up close.

4. Islands and Cays:

- The Great Barrier Reef is dotted with numerous islands and coral cays, offering unique experiences and opportunities for exploration.

- Heron Island, Lady Elliot Island, and Lizard Island are some of the notable islands within the reef, providing accommodation options and access to exceptional diving and snorkeling spots.

- The Whitsunday Islands, located within the Great Barrier Reef Marine Park, offer breathtaking beaches and access to the reef's wonders.

5. Conservation and Protection:

- The Great Barrier Reef is a UNESCO World Heritage site and is recognized for its ecological significance and global importance.

- Efforts are made to protect and preserve the reef through various initiatives, including the Great Barrier Reef Marine Park Authority, which manages and regulates activities within the marine park.

6. **Tourism and Activities:**

- The Great Barrier Reef attracts millions of visitors each year, offering a range of tourism activities and experiences.
- Snorkeling and scuba diving allow visitors to explore the coral reefs, encountering colorful fish, turtles, and other marine creatures.
- Boat tours, sailing trips, and scenic flights provide different perspectives and opportunities to appreciate the vastness and beauty of the reef.

7. **Climate Change and Conservation Efforts:**

- Climate change poses a significant threat to the Great Barrier Reef, with rising sea temperatures and ocean acidification impacting the health and resilience of the coral ecosystem.

  - Conservation efforts are focused on reef management, reducing pollution and runoff, and raising awareness about the importance of sustainability and protecting this fragile ecosystem.

The Great Barrier Reef is a globally significant natural wonder, offering unparalleled beauty, biodiversity, and unique experiences for visitors. It serves as a reminder of the importance of preserving and protecting our fragile marine ecosystems for future generations.

Outback Queensland

Outback Queensland is a vast and rugged region located in the inland areas of the Australian state of Queensland. It is known for its remote and sparsely populated landscapes, rich Indigenous culture, and unique outback experiences. Here are some details and information about Outback Queensland:

1. **Geography and Location:**

   - Outback Queensland encompasses a large portion of the state's inland, extending westward from the Great Dividing Range.

   - The region covers a vast area, spanning approximately 1.7 million square kilometers (656,377 square miles), making it larger than many countries.

   - It borders the Northern Territory to the west, South Australia to the southwest, and New South Wales to the south.

2. **Diverse Landscapes:**

- Outback Queensland is characterized by diverse landscapes, ranging from vast plains and red deserts to rocky gorges and sandstone formations.
- The region includes iconic natural landmarks such as the Simpson Desert, the Channel Country, the Diamantina National Park, and the Carnarvon Gorge.

3. Indigenous Culture and History:
- Outback Queensland has a rich Indigenous heritage, with a strong presence of Aboriginal and Torres Strait Islander cultures.
- Visitors have the opportunity to learn about the history, art, and traditions of the local Indigenous communities through cultural tours, art centers, and storytelling experiences.

4. Outback Towns and Communities:

- Outback Queensland is dotted with unique and historic towns that showcase the spirit and character of the region.
- Some notable towns include Longreach, Winton, Birdsville, Mount Isa, and Charleville.
- These towns offer a glimpse into the outback way of life, with museums, heritage sites, and events celebrating the region's history and culture.

5. Outback Experiences and Activities:
- Outback Queensland offers a range of unforgettable experiences for visitors.
- Adventure enthusiasts can embark on 4WD expeditions, camel treks, and guided bushwalking tours to explore the region's remote and rugged landscapes.
- The region is also known for its iconic outback events, including the Birdsville Races, the Big Red Bash music festival, and the Outback Queensland Masters golf tournament.

6. **Natural Wonders and National Parks**:

  - Outback Queensland is home to several stunning national parks and natural wonders.

  - Carnarvon Gorge, with its towering sandstone cliffs, ancient Aboriginal rock art, and picturesque walking trails, is a must-visit destination.

  - Other notable national parks include Diamantina National Park, Boodjamulla (Lawn Hill) National Park, and the Currawinya National Park, offering opportunities for wildlife spotting, birdwatching, and camping.

7. **Mining and Pastoral Industries:**

  - Outback Queensland has a significant presence of mining and pastoral industries, contributing to the region's economy.

  - Mount Isa is known for its mining operations, particularly for copper, lead, and zinc.

- Cattle and sheep farming are prominent in the region, with vast pastoral stations supporting the agricultural industry.

8. **Stargazing and Dark Sky Experiences**:
   - Outback Queensland's remote locations offer ideal conditions for stargazing and experiencing the brilliance of the night sky.
   - Several observatories and dedicated stargazing tours provide the opportunity to witness the stunning Southern Hemisphere constellations and celestial phenomena.

Outback Queensland offers a unique and authentic Australian outback experience, showcasing vast landscapes, rich Indigenous culture, and a sense of adventure. It is a destination that allows visitors to disconnect from the bustling city life and immerse themselves in the raw beauty and tranquility of the outback.

Attractions and Activities

Beaches and Coastal Escapes

Queensland, Australia is known for its stunning coastline and pristine beaches, offering a wide range of attractions and activities for beach lovers and those seeking coastal escapes. Here are some notable beaches and coastal destinations in Queensland:

1. **Gold Coast**: Located in the southeast corner of Queensland, the Gold Coast is renowned for its golden sandy beaches, vibrant nightlife, and world-class surfing spots. Some popular beaches in the area include Surfers Paradise Beach, Burleigh Heads Beach, and Coolangatta Beach. You can enjoy swimming, sunbathing, surfing, and beachside dining along the bustling coastline.

2. **Sunshine Coast**: Just north of the Gold Coast, the Sunshine Coast offers a more laid-back and relaxed beach experience. Noosa Main Beach, Mooloolaba Beach, and Kings Beach are among the top beaches in the region. Apart from swimming and sunbathing, you can explore the Noosa National Park, go whale watching, or enjoy water sports such as kayaking and paddleboarding.

3. **Great Barrier Reef**: Queensland is home to the iconic Great Barrier Reef, the world's largest coral reef system. While not technically a beach, the reef offers unparalleled opportunities for snorkeling, scuba diving, and boat tours. You can explore vibrant coral gardens, encounter diverse marine life, and even take part in conservation activities.

4. **Whitsunday Islands**: Located off the coast of central Queensland, the Whitsunday Islands are a tropical paradise known for their stunning white-sand beaches and crystal-clear waters. Whitehaven Beach, with its pristine silica sand and dazzling turquoise waters, is a highlight. You can also go sailing, snorkeling, or enjoy scenic hikes on the islands.

5. **Fraser Island**: As the largest sand island in the world, Fraser Island offers a unique coastal experience. You can drive along the sandy beaches, swim in crystal-clear freshwater lakes, and explore the lush rainforests. Don't miss the famous Lake McKenzie, Eli Creek, and the Maheno Shipwreck while you're there.

6. **Cairns and Tropical North Queensland**: Cairns serves as a gateway to the Great Barrier Reef and the lush rainforests of Tropical

North Queensland. Palm Cove, Trinity Beach, and Port Douglas are some of the popular coastal destinations in the region. Besides beach activities, you can take scenic helicopter rides, visit the Daintree Rainforest, or go on an Aboriginal cultural tour.

7. **Moreton Island**: Situated off the coast of Brisbane, Moreton Island is a haven for nature lovers and adventure seekers. Tangalooma Beach, known for its wild dolphin feeding experiences, is a major attraction. You can also explore the island's sand dunes, snorkel around the Tangalooma Wrecks, or go on a thrilling quad bike tour.

These are just a few examples of the many incredible beaches and coastal escapes Queensland has to offer. Whether you're seeking relaxation, adventure, or natural beauty, Queensland's coastline promises a memorable experience for visitors of all kinds.

Queensland, Australia boasts a diverse range of national parks and lush rainforests, offering nature enthusiasts and adventure seekers a wealth of attractions and activities to explore. Here are some notable national parks and rainforests in Queensland:

1. **Daintree National Park**: Located in Tropical North Queensland, the Daintree National Park is a UNESCO World Heritage-listed site and one of the oldest rainforests on Earth. It is home to an incredible array of flora and fauna, including rare and endangered species. Visitors can take guided walks through the dense rainforest, go on river cruises, or embark on thrilling zip line adventures.

2. **Lamington National Park**: Situated in the Gold Coast hinterland, Lamington National Park is renowned for its stunning landscapes, ancient rainforests, and abundant wildlife.

79

The park offers numerous walking trails, ranging from easy strolls to challenging hikes. The Tree Top Walkway provides a unique perspective on the rainforest canopy, and birdwatching enthusiasts will be delighted by the diverse birdlife in the area.

3. **Girraween National Park**: Located on the Queensland-NSW border, Girraween National Park is famous for its granite landscapes and distinctive balancing boulders. Visitors can enjoy scenic walks, rock climbing, and wildlife spotting. The park is particularly beautiful during spring when wildflowers bloom, adding vibrant colors to the already stunning surroundings.

4. **Springbrook National Park**: Situated in the Gold Coast hinterland, Springbrook National Park is a haven of waterfalls, lush rainforests, and ancient trees. The park offers a variety of walking trails, including the popular Twin

Falls Circuit and the Natural Bridge walk, where you can witness a stunning waterfall cascading through a naturally formed arch. At night, the park's unique glow worms illuminate the rainforest.

5. **Hinchinbrook Island National Park**: Hinchinbrook Island, located off the coast of Townsville, is the largest island national park in Australia. With its rugged mountains, pristine beaches, and mangrove-lined waterways, it offers a true wilderness experience. Visitors can hike the Thorsborne Trail, a challenging multi-day trek that takes you through diverse ecosystems and offers breathtaking views.

6. **Carnarvon Gorge**: Situated in Carnarvon National Park, Carnarvon Gorge is a natural oasis in the heart of Queensland's Outback. The gorge is known for its towering sandstone cliffs, ancient Aboriginal rock art, and

picturesque waterholes. Visitors can explore the gorge through a network of walking trails, discovering unique rock formations, waterfalls, and abundant wildlife along the way.

7. **Mount Tamborine**: Located in the Gold Coast hinterland, Mount Tamborine offers a mix of subtropical rainforests, panoramic views, and charming village vibes. The area is known for its lush walking trails, scenic lookouts, and cascading waterfalls. Visitors can also indulge in local produce, boutique wineries, and art galleries in the quaint township.

These are just a few examples of the incredible national parks and rainforests you can explore in Queensland. Each destination offers its own unique natural beauty, biodiversity, and opportunities for adventure, making it a paradise for nature lovers and outdoor enthusiasts.

Wildlife Encounters

Queensland, Australia is teeming with unique and diverse wildlife, providing ample opportunities for unforgettable wildlife encounters. From cuddly koalas to elusive cassowaries, here are some notable attractions and activities in Queensland for wildlife enthusiasts:

1. **Australia Zoo:** Located on the Sunshine Coast, Australia Zoo is one of the country's most renowned wildlife conservation parks. Founded by the late Steve Irwin, it offers an up-close experience with a wide range of animals, including kangaroos, wombats, crocodiles, and a variety of reptiles. The zoo's Wildlife Warriors show provides an exciting demonstration of wildlife conservation efforts.

2. **Lone Pine Koala Sanctuary**: Situated in Brisbane, Lone Pine Koala Sanctuary is the

world's oldest and largest koala sanctuary. Visitors can cuddle koalas and have their photo taken, as well as hand-feed kangaroos and encounter other native Australian wildlife such as platypuses, wombats, and emus. Daily animal shows and presentations provide educational and entertaining experiences.

3. **Lady Elliot Island**: Located in the southern Great Barrier Reef, Lady Elliot Island is a haven for marine wildlife. Snorkeling and scuba diving opportunities allow visitors to swim alongside majestic manta rays, turtles, and colorful tropical fish. The island is also a significant nesting site for green and loggerhead turtles, providing a chance to witness their nesting and hatching activities.

4. **Magnetic Island**: Just off the coast of Townsville, Magnetic Island is home to an abundance of wildlife, including koalas, rock wallabies, and a variety of bird species. The

island's national park offers hiking trails where visitors can spot these animals in their natural habitats. The Bungalow Bay Koala Village offers guided tours and interactive experiences with koalas and other native wildlife.

5. **Currumbin Wildlife Sanctuary**: Situated on the Gold Coast, Currumbin Wildlife Sanctuary allows visitors to get up close and personal with a range of Australian animals. You can hand-feed kangaroos, cuddle koalas, and watch interactive wildlife shows featuring birds of prey, crocodiles, and snakes. The sanctuary also offers treetop rope courses and ziplining for added adventure.

6. **Mossman Gorge**: Located in the Daintree Rainforest, Mossman Gorge provides an opportunity to encounter unique wildlife in a pristine natural setting. Visitors can take guided walks through the rainforest, where

they may spot cassowaries, colorful birds, tree-dwelling marsupials, and a variety of reptiles and insects.

7. **Tjapukai Aboriginal Cultural Park**: Situated near Cairns, Tjapukai Aboriginal Cultural Park offers an immersive cultural experience while also showcasing native wildlife. Visitors can learn about the indigenous culture through dance performances, didgeridoo playing, and interactive activities. The park's Wildlife Park allows visitors to meet kangaroos, wallabies, and other native animals.

These are just a few examples of the many wildlife attractions and activities available in Queensland. Whether you're fascinated by koalas, marine life, or the unique animals of the rainforest, Queensland provides ample opportunities to experience Australia's remarkable wildlife up close.

Adventure and Outdoor Activities

Queensland, Australia is a paradise for adventure and outdoor enthusiasts, offering a wide range of thrilling activities and attractions. From adrenaline-pumping experiences to breathtaking natural wonders, here are some notable adventure and outdoor activities in Queensland:

1. **Great Barrier Reef**: Exploring the Great Barrier Reef is a must-do adventure in Queensland. Snorkeling or scuba diving allows you to witness the vibrant coral formations, swim alongside tropical fish, and encounter marine creatures such as turtles, reef sharks, and colorful reef systems. There are various operators offering reef tours departing from locations such as Cairns, Port Douglas, and the Whitsunday Islands.

2. **Skydiving**: Experience the ultimate thrill by skydiving over some of Queensland's most scenic locations. With breathtaking views of the coastline or rainforests, tandem skydiving allows you to freefall from thousands of feet and enjoy a bird's-eye perspective before landing safely on the ground. Popular skydiving locations include Cairns, Mission Beach, and the Sunshine Coast.

3. **White Water Rafting:** Queensland's rivers offer exhilarating white water rafting experiences suitable for both beginners and experienced rafters. The Tully River near Cairns is renowned for its challenging rapids, while the Barron River and the Russell River also provide exciting rafting adventures. Navigate the rapids, work as a team, and soak in the beautiful scenery along the way.

4. **Surfing**: With its pristine beaches and world-class waves, Queensland is a surfer's

paradise. Destinations like the Gold Coast, Sunshine Coast, and Noosa are known for their consistent surf breaks catering to all levels of experience. Take a surfing lesson or join a surf camp to catch the perfect wave and enjoy the exhilaration of riding the ocean swells.

5. **Hiking and Bushwalking**: Queensland's diverse landscapes offer a plethora of hiking and bushwalking trails for all levels of fitness. Explore the ancient rainforests of the Daintree National Park, hike the rugged trails of the Scenic Rim, or conquer the challenging peaks of the Glass House Mountains. The Great Walks of Queensland, such as the Thorsborne Trail and the Cooloola Great Walk, provide multi-day adventures through stunning natural environments.

6. **Bungee Jumping:** Get your adrenaline pumping by taking a leap of faith with a

bungee jump. The AJ Hackett Cairns Bungy site offers a thrilling 50-meter jump over a rainforest-fringed pond, while the Gold Coast's SkyPoint Climb includes an option to take a 270-meter high SkyPoint Bungy leap.

7. **Zip-lining and Canopy Tours**: Experience the thrill of zip-lining through Queensland's lush rainforests. Canopy tours and zip-line adventures are available in various locations, including the Daintree Rainforest, Gold Coast hinterland, and Tamborine Mountain. Soar through the treetops, enjoying panoramic views and a unique perspective on the surrounding nature.

8. **Hot Air Ballooning**: Take to the skies in a hot air balloon for a serene and breathtaking adventure. Float above the scenic landscapes of the Gold Coast, Cairns, or the Atherton Tablelands during a sunrise or sunset flight. Enjoy stunning aerial views of the coast,

mountains, and countryside as you experience the tranquility of hot air ballooning.

These are just a few examples of the thrilling adventure and outdoor activities available in Queensland. Whether you seek adrenaline-pumping experiences or a connection with nature, Queensland's diverse landscapes offer something for everyone's adventurous spirit.

Cultural and Historical Sites

Queensland, Australia is rich in cultural and historical sites that offer visitors a glimpse into the region's vibrant past and diverse heritage. From indigenous cultural centers to historic landmarks, here are some notable attractions and activities in Queensland for those interested in exploring the cultural and historical aspects of the region:

1. **Queensland Cultural Centre (Brisbane):** Located in South Bank, the Queensland Cultural Centre is a hub of cultural institutions. It houses the Queensland Museum, which offers exhibitions on natural history, science, and indigenous culture. The Queensland Art Gallery showcases a vast collection of Australian and international art, while the Gallery of Modern Art features contemporary artworks. The State Library of Queensland provides insights into the state's history and heritage.

2. **Tjapukai Aboriginal Cultural Park (Cairns):** Tjapukai Aboriginal Cultural Park offers visitors a chance to learn about the indigenous culture and heritage of the local Djabugay people. Engage in interactive experiences, such as traditional dance performances, didgeridoo playing, and bush tucker demonstrations. You can also try your hand at boomerang throwing and spear-throwing or take part in cultural workshops.

3. **Paronella Park (Mena Creek):** Paronella Park is a unique heritage site located in the tropical rainforest near Innisfail. It features the ruins of a Spanish-inspired castle built in the 1930s, surrounded by lush gardens and waterfalls. Explore the grounds, take a guided tour, and learn about the fascinating history of the park and its creator, José Paronella.

4. Port Arthur (Brisbane): Located on the tip of the Cape York Peninsula, Port Arthur is a historic settlement with a rich maritime heritage. It was once a thriving port during the gold rush era. Today, visitors can explore the restored buildings, including the customs house, cemetery, and stone church. Take a guided tour to learn about the area's history and maritime significance.

5. Cooktown History Centre (Cooktown): Cooktown, a town with significant historical importance, was where Captain James Cook first made landfall in Australia in 1770. The Cooktown History Centre showcases artifacts, photographs, and exhibits that depict the town's history, including its Aboriginal heritage and the impact of European settlement.

6. Museum of Tropical Queensland (Townsville): The Museum of Tropical

Queensland offers insights into the natural and cultural history of the region. It houses exhibits on the Great Barrier Reef, shipwrecks, and the heritage of North Queensland. One of the museum's highlights is the display of artifacts recovered from the wreck of HMS Pandora, which sank in 1791.

7. **Abbey Museum of Art and Archaeology (Caboolture):** The Abbey Museum displays a vast collection of art and artifacts from various cultures and time periods. Explore exhibits that span ancient Egypt, the Middle Ages, and Renaissance Europe. The museum also hosts reenactments, workshops, and events throughout the year.

These are just a few examples of the cultural and historical attractions and activities available in Queensland. Whether you're interested in indigenous culture, colonial history, or art and archaeology, Queensland's diverse range of sites provides a fascinating journey through time and heritage.

Food and Wine Experiences

Queensland, Australia offers a delightful array of food and wine experiences, showcasing the region's diverse culinary scene and vibrant local produce. From farm-to-table dining to wine tastings, here are some notable attractions and activities in Queensland for food and wine enthusiasts:

1. **Granite Belt Wine Country (Stanthorpe)**: Located in the beautiful Granite Belt region, known for its cool climate, Granite Belt Wine Country is a haven for wine lovers. Discover award-winning wineries and cellar doors offering tastings of the region's acclaimed wines, particularly its signature varietals such as Shiraz, Cabernet Sauvignon, and Verdelho. The area is also known for its gourmet food offerings, including locally produced cheeses and fresh produce.

2. Bundaberg Rum Distillery (Bundaberg):
Visit the Bundaberg Rum Distillery, where Australia's iconic Bundaberg Rum is produced. Take a guided tour to learn about the rum-making process, explore the museum showcasing the brand's history, and indulge in a tasting session to savor the distinct flavors of this beloved spirit.

3. Eat Street Northshore (Brisbane): Located on the banks of the Brisbane River, Eat Street Northshore is a vibrant market precinct offering a diverse range of food stalls and vendors. Sample a variety of cuisines, from international street food to gourmet desserts, while enjoying live music and a lively atmosphere.

4. Noosa Food and Wine Festival (Noosa):
Held annually in Noosa, the Noosa Food and Wine Festival is a premier culinary event showcasing the best of local and national

chefs, winemakers, and producers. Attend cooking demonstrations, wine tastings, and foodie events, and indulge in the flavors of the region's fresh seafood, tropical fruits, and artisanal products.

5. **The Ginger Factory (Yandina):** Located on the Sunshine Coast, the Ginger Factory is a delightful attraction dedicated to all things ginger. Take a guided tour to learn about the cultivation and processing of ginger, taste a variety of ginger-based products, and enjoy a meal at the Ginger Café, which offers a range of ginger-infused dishes.

6. **Eumundi Markets (Eumundi):** Eumundi Markets, held on Wednesdays and Saturdays, is one of Australia's largest and most renowned artisan markets. Stroll through the stalls to discover a wide range of locally made products, including gourmet food items, fresh produce, and handcrafted treats. Enjoy live

music and entertainment as you explore this
bustling market.

7. **Farm-to-Table Experiences**: Queensland's
fertile lands provide opportunities for
farm-to-table experiences. Many regions
offer the chance to visit working farms, where
you can pick your own fresh produce, learn
about sustainable farming practices, and
enjoy farm-fresh meals prepared by talented
chefs.

8. **Seafood Experiences:** Being located along
Australia's coastline, Queensland is renowned
for its seafood. From beachside fish and chips
to upscale seafood restaurants, there are
plenty of options to savor the flavors of locally
caught fish, prawns, oysters, and more.

These are just a few examples of the food and
wine experiences available in Queensland.
Whether you're a wine connoisseur, a food

lover, or simply enjoy discovering local
flavors, Queensland's culinary scene offers a
delightful journey for your taste buds.

Shopping and Entertainment

Queensland, Australia offers a wide range of shopping and entertainment options, from vibrant markets and shopping precincts to entertainment hubs that cater to various interests. Here are some notable attractions and activities in Queensland for shopping and entertainment:

1. **Queen Street Mall (Brisbane):** Located in the heart of Brisbane's CBD, Queen Street Mall is a bustling pedestrian mall known for its excellent shopping opportunities. Explore a variety of fashion boutiques, department stores, specialty shops, and major retail brands. The mall is also home to entertainment venues, cinemas, and a vibrant selection of cafes and restaurants.

2. **Pacific Fair Shopping Centre (Gold Coast):** Pacific Fair is one of Queensland's largest shopping centers and a premier shopping

destination on the Gold Coast. It features over 400 stores, including high-end fashion brands, designer boutiques, homeware stores, and specialty shops. The center also offers a range of dining options and entertainment facilities, including a cinema complex and an outdoor dining precinct.

3. **Harbour Town Outlet Shopping Centre (Gold Coast):** For bargain hunters and fashion enthusiasts, Harbour Town is a popular choice. Located on the Gold Coast, it offers a wide range of outlet stores, selling discounted designer brands, fashion, accessories, and homewares. Enjoy substantial savings while exploring the center's diverse retail offerings.

4. **South Bank Parklands (Brisbane):** South Bank Parklands is a vibrant entertainment precinct situated on the Brisbane River. Along with beautiful parklands and stunning river views, it boasts an array of dining options,

from casual eateries to upscale restaurants. The precinct is also home to the Queensland Performing Arts Centre (QPAC), which hosts a variety of theater performances, concerts, and cultural events throughout the year.

5. **Night Markets (Various Locations):** Queensland's night markets offer a unique shopping and entertainment experience. From the Eat Street Northshore in Brisbane to the Surfers Paradise Beachfront Markets on the Gold Coast, these markets come alive in the evenings, offering a wide range of food stalls, artisan products, live music, and a bustling atmosphere.

6. **Cairns Night Markets (Cairns):** Located in the heart of Cairns, the Cairns Night Markets are a popular attraction for tourists and locals alike. Open every night, these markets offer a vast array of stalls selling souvenirs, clothing, jewelry, and local handicrafts. Take your time

to explore the various stalls and enjoy the lively atmosphere.

7. **Theme Parks (Gold Coast):** The Gold Coast is renowned for its world-class theme parks, providing entertainment for all ages. Visit Warner Bros. Movie World to experience thrilling rides and meet your favorite characters, explore the marine life at Sea World, or enjoy the water slides and attractions at Wet'n'Wild. Dreamworld and WhiteWater World are also popular choices for adrenaline-pumping rides and water-based fun.

8. **Arts and Cultural Centers**: Queensland is home to several arts and cultural centers, such as the Queensland Performing Arts Centre (QPAC) in Brisbane and the Cairns Performing Arts Centre (CPAC) in Cairns. These venues host a wide range of performances, including

theater productions, ballet, dance shows, concerts, and art exhibitions.

These are just a few examples of the shopping and entertainment attractions and activities available in Queensland. Whether you're looking for retail therapy, vibrant markets, live performances, or theme park adventures, Queensland has something to offer for everyone's interests and preferences.

Accommodation Options

Hotels and Resorts

Queensland, Australia, is known for its stunning natural landscapes, vibrant cities, and pristine coastline. Whether you're planning a relaxing beach vacation, exploring the Great Barrier Reef, or embarking on an adventure in the Queensland outback, the state offers a wide range of accommodation options, including hotels and resorts. Here are some details and information on accommodation options in Queensland:

1. **Luxury Resorts:**
   - Qualia Resort: Located on Hamilton Island in the Whitsundays, Qualia offers luxurious private pavilions with stunning ocean views, infinity pools, and world-class amenities.
   - Palazzo Versace: Situated on the Gold Coast, this opulent resort combines Italian

elegance with Australian coastal beauty. It features spacious rooms, a private marina, and exquisite dining options.

2. **Beachfront Hotels:**

   - Sheraton Mirage Resort & Spa: Nestled along the Gold Coast's pristine beaches, this hotel offers spacious rooms with ocean views, a lagoon-style pool, and a luxurious spa.

   - Peppers Noosa Resort & Villas: Located in Noosa Heads, this hotel provides stylish accommodation with direct access to Noosa's Main Beach. It features a day spa, multiple swimming pools, and lush gardens.

3. **Rainforest Retreats:**

   - Silky Oaks Lodge: Situated in the Daintree Rainforest, this eco-lodge offers secluded treehouses and riverfront villas. Guests can enjoy rainforest walks, spa treatments, and gourmet dining experiences.

- O'Reilly's Rainforest Retreat: Tucked away in the Lamington National Park, this retreat offers a range of accommodation options, including rainforest villas and cozy guesthouses. It provides guided bird walks, treetop canopy tours, and breathtaking views.

4. City Hotels:

- Sofitel Brisbane Central: Located in the heart of Brisbane, this elegant hotel offers luxurious rooms, a rooftop pool, and a variety of dining options. It provides easy access to the city's attractions and shopping precincts.

- Hilton Cairns: Situated on the Cairns waterfront, this hotel offers stylish rooms with stunning ocean or city views. It features a rooftop pool, a spa, and proximity to the Great Barrier Reef departure points.

5. Island Resorts:

- Hayman Island Resort: Found in the Whitsundays, this resort offers contemporary rooms, beachfront villas, and private residences. Guests can indulge in water sports, spa treatments, and explore the surrounding coral reefs.

- Lizard Island Resort: Located on a secluded island on the Great Barrier Reef, this exclusive resort offers luxurious suites and private villas with breathtaking ocean views. It offers world-class diving and snorkeling experiences.

It's important to note that availability, prices, and additional amenities can vary depending on the season and specific locations. It's advisable to check with individual hotels and resorts for the most up-to-date information and to make reservations in advance.

Apartments and Holiday Homes

Queensland, Australia, offers a wide range of apartment rentals and holiday homes, providing flexibility, space, and a home-away-from-home experience for travelers. Whether you're looking for a beachside apartment or a spacious holiday home in the hinterland, Queensland has plenty of options to suit various preferences and budgets. Here are some details and information on accommodation options in Queensland for apartments and holiday homes:

1. **Beachside Apartments:**
   - Surfers Paradise Apartments (Gold Coast): Located in the heart of Surfers Paradise, these apartments offer stunning ocean views, self-contained units with kitchens, and access to resort-style amenities such as pools, gyms, and BBQ areas.

- Palm Cove Apartments (Palm Cove): Situated in the idyllic Palm Cove, these apartments provide a tropical escape with close proximity to the beach. They feature spacious living areas, private balconies, and access to pools and landscaped gardens.

2. **City Apartments**:
- Brisbane City Apartments (Brisbane): Offering a range of apartments in the central business district, these accommodations provide convenient access to Brisbane's attractions, shopping, and dining. They feature modern amenities, fully equipped kitchens, and some may offer onsite gyms or pools.
- Cairns Esplanade Apartments (Cairns): Located along the scenic Cairns Esplanade, these apartments offer spacious living areas, balconies with ocean or city views, and access to swimming pools. They provide a

convenient base for exploring the Great Barrier Reef and the Daintree Rainforest.

3. **Holiday Homes**:
  - Noosa Holiday Homes (Noosa): With a range of holiday homes available, Noosa offers options for families or larger groups. These homes often feature multiple bedrooms, private pools, outdoor entertaining areas, and proximity to Noosa's beaches and national parks.
  - Port Douglas Holiday Homes (Port Douglas): Whether nestled in lush rainforest or near Four Mile Beach, Port Douglas offers holiday homes with a tropical ambiance. These homes typically offer spacious interiors, outdoor spaces, and private pools, making them ideal for a relaxing getaway.

4. **Hinterland Retreats:**
  - Montville Holiday Homes (Montville): Located in the beautiful Sunshine Coast

Hinterland, Montville offers holiday homes surrounded by scenic views and rainforest. These retreats provide a tranquil setting, often with spacious interiors, cozy fireplaces, and outdoor areas to enjoy the serenity.

- Tamborine Mountain Accommodation (Tamborine Mountain): Situated in the Gold Coast Hinterland, Tamborine Mountain offers holiday homes amidst picturesque landscapes. These accommodations often feature rustic charm, breathtaking views, and easy access to wineries, rainforest walks, and local attractions.

It's advisable to check with individual providers or reputable accommodation websites to find the most suitable apartment or holiday home for your needs. Availability, prices, and specific amenities can vary, so it's recommended to book in advance, especially during peak travel seasons.

Bed and Breakfasts

Queensland, Australia, offers a charming selection of bed and breakfast accommodations that provide a more intimate and personalized experience for travelers. These establishments often feature comfortable rooms, delicious breakfast options, and warm hospitality. Here are some details and information on bed and breakfast options in Queensland:

1. Narrows Escape Rainforest Retreat (Montville):

   - Situated in the Sunshine Coast Hinterland, this retreat offers private cottages nestled within the rainforest. Guests can enjoy spacious accommodation with fireplaces, spa baths, and private decks. A gourmet breakfast is delivered to the cottage each morning.

2. Hillcrest Mountain View Retreat (Maleny):

- Overlooking the stunning Glass House Mountains, this retreat offers boutique accommodation in a peaceful setting. Guests can relax in beautifully appointed rooms, enjoy panoramic views, and savor a hearty breakfast made from local produce.

3. **Atherton Blue Gum B&B (Atherton):**
   - Located in the heart of the Atherton Tablelands, this bed and breakfast is surrounded by tropical gardens. It offers comfortable rooms with private balconies, a guest lounge with a fireplace, and a delicious breakfast featuring homemade bread and local ingredients.

4. **Mango Hill Farm (Yandina):**
   - Situated on a picturesque farm in the Sunshine Coast region, Mango Hill offers a unique farm stay experience. Guests can stay in self-contained cottages or rooms in the main house, enjoy farm activities, pick fresh

fruit, and indulge in a hearty farm-style breakfast.

5. **Port Douglas Valley Retreat (Port Douglas):**
   - This peaceful retreat is nestled in the Mowbray Valley, a short drive from Port Douglas. It offers comfortable rooms with private entrances, access to a swimming pool and spa, and a delicious breakfast served on the veranda with stunning views of the rainforest.

6. **Ravensbourne Escape (Ravensbourne):**
   - Located in the scenic Ravensbourne National Park, this retreat offers self-contained cottages and stylish suites. Guests can enjoy the tranquility of the surrounding bushland, take bushwalks, relax in a private hot tub, and savor a continental or cooked breakfast.

These bed and breakfast options in Queensland provide an intimate and cozy atmosphere, allowing guests to connect with the local surroundings and enjoy personalized service. It's recommended to check with each establishment for availability, specific amenities, and booking details, as they can vary.

Camping and Caravan Parks

Queensland, Australia, is a haven for camping and caravan enthusiasts, offering a wide array of camping grounds and caravan parks that cater to different preferences and budgets. Whether you prefer a coastal camping experience or a scenic bush retreat, Queensland has numerous options to choose from. Here are some details and information on camping and caravan park options in Queensland:

1. **Coastal Camping**:
   - Dicky Beach Family Holiday Park (Caloundra): Situated on the Sunshine Coast, this beachfront caravan park offers powered and unpowered sites, as well as cabin accommodation. Guests can enjoy direct beach access, facilities such as BBQ areas, a camp kitchen, and a playground.
   - Inskip Peninsula Recreation Area (Rainbow Beach): Located near Rainbow Beach, this

coastal camping area provides beachfront camping sites with beautiful views. It is a popular spot for fishing, boating, and exploring the nearby Fraser Island.

2. **National Park Camping**:
   - Main Range National Park (Cunningham's Gap): This national park offers several camping areas within picturesque surroundings. Campers can enjoy bushwalking, birdwatching, and stunning views of the Great Dividing Range.
   - Boodjamulla (Lawn Hill) National Park (Mount Isa): Nestled in the rugged outback, this national park provides camping options near the stunning Lawn Hill Gorge. Visitors can experience canoeing, bushwalking, and swimming in the crystal-clear waters.

3. **Hinterland Camping**:
   - Lake Somerset Holiday Park (Kilcoy): Located near Somerset Dam in the Brisbane

Valley, this holiday park offers powered and unpowered camping sites, as well as cabins. Activities include fishing, boating, water sports, and hiking in the surrounding area.

- Binna Burra Campsite (Lamington National Park): Situated in the World Heritage-listed Lamington National Park, this campsite offers a true rainforest camping experience. Campers can explore walking trails, spot wildlife, and immerse themselves in the lush surroundings.

4. Caravan Parks:

- BIG4 Adventure Whitsunday Resort (Airlie Beach): This award-winning resort offers caravan and camping sites with excellent facilities, including pools, water slides, mini-golf, and a range of recreational activities. It's an ideal base for exploring the Whitsunday Islands and the Great Barrier Reef.

- Cairns Coconut Holiday Resort (Cairns): Known as one of Australia's top-rated caravan parks, this resort offers spacious sites, resort-style pools, water slides, and a wide range of amenities and activities for the whole family.

When planning a camping or caravan trip in Queensland, it's essential to check the availability of sites, any permit requirements, and the specific facilities offered at each location. It's also recommended to consider the season and make reservations in advance, especially during peak travel periods.

Dining and Cuisine

Local Delicacies

Queensland, Australia, offers a diverse culinary scene that showcases a variety of local delicacies. With its abundance of fresh produce, coastal seafood, and multicultural influences, Queensland's dining options are sure to tantalize your taste buds. Here are some local delicacies you can savor in Queensland:

1. **Moreton Bay Bugs:** Moreton Bay Bugs are a prized seafood delicacy native to the waters of Moreton Bay in Queensland. These crustaceans resemble small lobsters and have a sweet and delicate flavor. They are often grilled, barbecued, or used in seafood dishes like bugs thermidor.

2. **Barramundi**: Barramundi is a popular fish found in Queensland's coastal waters. Known for its firm, white flesh and mild flavor, barramundi is a versatile ingredient in many seafood dishes. It can be steamed, grilled, fried, or used in curries and stews.

3. **Macadamia Nuts**: Queensland is the largest producer of macadamia nuts in Australia. These native nuts have a rich, buttery flavor and are often used in both sweet and savory dishes. You can find them in desserts, salads, roasted snacks, or even incorporated into sauces and marinades.

4. **Pawpaw (Papaya)**: Queensland's warm climate provides the perfect conditions for growing delicious pawpaw fruits. Pawpaws are known for their vibrant orange flesh and sweet, tropical taste. They are commonly eaten fresh or used in salads, smoothies, and desserts.

5. **Mangoes**: Queensland's mangoes are renowned for their juicy, sweet flavor. During the summer months, you'll find an abundance of mangoes in markets and roadside stalls. Enjoy them fresh, make mango salsas, chutneys, or indulge in mango-flavored desserts like mango cheesecake or mango ice cream.

6. **Mud Crab**: Queensland's mud crabs are highly sought after for their succulent meat. These crabs are often steamed, stir-fried, or used in popular dishes like chili mud crab or salt and pepper mud crab. The tender and sweet crab meat is a true delicacy.

7. **Native Australian Bush Tucker**: Queensland is home to a rich variety of native Australian ingredients known as bush tucker. These include ingredients like finger limes, quandong (native peach), wattleseed, lemon

myrtle, and kangaroo meat. Many restaurants in Queensland incorporate these unique ingredients into their dishes, offering a taste of Australia's indigenous culinary heritage.

When visiting Queensland, be sure to explore the local markets, seafood restaurants, and farm-to-table eateries to fully experience the state's vibrant dining scene. Whether you're a seafood lover, a fan of tropical fruits, or an adventurous eater seeking unique flavors, Queensland's local delicacies are sure to satisfy your cravings.

Fine Dining

Queensland offers a plethora of options for fine dining, catering to those seeking exceptional culinary experiences. From award-winning restaurants to stunning waterfront venues, here are some details and information on fine dining in Queensland:

1. **Brisbane Fine Dining:** Brisbane, the capital city of Queensland, boasts a vibrant fine dining scene. The city is home to numerous renowned restaurants that offer innovative and sophisticated menus crafted by talented chefs. From modern Australian cuisine to international flavors, you'll find a range of dining options to suit your preferences. Some popular fine dining establishments in Brisbane include Esquire, Urbane, and Aria Brisbane.

2. **Gold Coast Gastronomy:** The Gold Coast is renowned for its stunning beaches and

vibrant nightlife, and it also offers a diverse fine dining scene. Surfers Paradise and Broadbeach are particularly known for their upscale dining options. You can indulge in world-class seafood, modern Australian cuisine, and international flavors while enjoying breathtaking views of the coastline. Notable fine dining venues on the Gold Coast include Hellenika, Kiyomi, and The Fish House.

3. **Noosa's Culinary Delights**: Noosa, located on the Sunshine Coast of Queensland, is a popular destination for food enthusiasts. The town's picturesque setting and thriving food scene make it a must-visit for those seeking fine dining experiences. Noosa is known for its emphasis on fresh local produce, with many restaurants offering farm-to-table menus. Locale, Wasabi, and Ricky's River Bar & Restaurant are highly regarded fine dining establishments in Noosa.

4. **Tropical Dining in Cairns**: Cairns, a gateway to the Great Barrier Reef, offers a unique dining experience infused with tropical flavors. The city's proximity to the ocean ensures an abundance of fresh seafood, and its multicultural influences result in a diverse culinary landscape. Cairns is home to a range of fine dining establishments, including Ochre Restaurant, Tamarind, and Salt House, where you can savor innovative dishes and enjoy stunning waterfront views.

5. **Hinterland Retreats:** Queensland's hinterland regions, such as the Scenic Rim and the Sunshine Coast Hinterland, provide an idyllic setting for indulging in fine dining. These areas are known for their boutique restaurants set amidst breathtaking natural landscapes. You can savor locally sourced ingredients, artisanal wines, and inventive menus showcasing the region's produce.

Some notable hinterland dining destinations include The Peak at Spicers Peak Lodge, The Long Apron at Spicers Clovelly Estate, and The Terrace of Maleny.

When dining at fine establishments in Queensland, it is advisable to make reservations in advance, as these restaurants often have limited seating due to their popularity. Additionally, many fine dining venues offer degustation menus, wine pairings, and impeccable service to enhance your overall dining experience.

Casual Eateries and Street Food

Queensland offers a vibrant food scene that extends beyond fine dining. If you're looking for casual eateries and street food options, you'll find an array of delicious choices throughout the state. Here are some details and information on casual eateries and street food in Queensland:

1. **Food Trucks and Markets:** Queensland is home to a thriving food truck culture and bustling markets where you can discover a wide range of culinary delights. Cities like Brisbane, Gold Coast, and Cairns host regular food truck events and markets, featuring an assortment of cuisines such as gourmet burgers, tacos, Asian fusion, wood-fired pizza, and more. Some popular markets to explore include Eat Street Northshore in Brisbane, NightQuarter on the Gold Coast, and Rusty's Market in Cairns.

2. **Beachside Cafes:** With its stunning coastline, Queensland offers numerous beachside cafes where you can enjoy a relaxed meal with ocean views. From the Sunshine Coast to the Gold Coast and beyond, you'll find cafes serving up fresh seafood, hearty breakfasts, and light bites. These cafes often embrace a laid-back atmosphere, making them the perfect spot to unwind after a day of beach activities. Some notable beachside cafes include Three Blue Ducks at The Farm in Byron Bay (near the Queensland border), The Nook Espresso Bar in Burleigh Heads, and Mooloolaba Esplanade in Mooloolaba.

3. **Urban Laneways and Precincts**: Queensland's cities are dotted with vibrant laneways and precincts that host a variety of casual eateries and street food vendors. For example, in Brisbane, you can explore Fish Lane, a trendy laneway filled with hip cafes, bars, and street food stalls. Additionally, the

Fortitude Valley and West End neighborhoods in Brisbane are known for their multicultural dining scenes, offering diverse cuisines from around the world.

4. **Surf Clubs and Pubs**: Queensland's surf clubs and pubs are popular gathering spots where you can enjoy casual dining with a relaxed atmosphere. These venues often offer classic pub fare, seafood platters, and refreshing beverages. Whether you're looking for a casual lunch, dinner, or a sunset drink, surf clubs and pubs along the coastline provide a quintessential Queensland experience. Check out venues like North Burleigh Surf Life Saving Club, The Spotted Cow in Toowoomba, or The Regatta Hotel in Brisbane.

5. **Ethnic Enclaves**: Queensland is a melting pot of cultures, and its cities are home to various ethnic enclaves where you can find

authentic street food and casual dining options. Areas like Fortitude Valley in Brisbane, Southport in the Gold Coast, and Cairns' city center are known for their multicultural culinary scenes, offering cuisines ranging from Thai and Vietnamese to Indian and Middle Eastern.

Whether you're grabbing a quick bite from a food truck, exploring local markets, enjoying a meal at a beachside cafe, or savoring international flavors in urban precincts, Queensland's casual eateries and street food scene will satisfy your cravings for tasty and diverse fare.

Cafés and Bakeries

Queensland is home to a plethora of charming cafés and bakeries that cater to coffee aficionados and pastry enthusiasts alike. Whether you're in search of a cozy spot for a cup of freshly brewed coffee or craving delectable pastries and baked goods, you'll find a range of delightful options throughout the state. Here are some details and information on cafés and bakeries in Queensland:

1. **Brisbane's Café Culture:** Brisbane, the capital city of Queensland, boasts a thriving café culture with an abundance of unique and stylish establishments. From specialty coffee shops to trendy brunch spots, Brisbane offers a diverse range of cafés to suit all tastes. You can find cafes tucked away in laneways, nestled in leafy suburbs, or boasting panoramic city views. Some notable cafés in

Brisbane include Campos Coffee, Strauss Café, and The Single Guys Coffee Co.

2. **Coastal Gems**: Queensland's coastal regions are dotted with charming cafés that provide a perfect backdrop for enjoying a cup of coffee or indulging in freshly baked treats. Whether you're in the Gold Coast, Sunshine Coast, or Cairns, you'll find seaside cafés that offer stunning views of the ocean and a relaxed atmosphere. These coastal cafés often feature menus with a focus on fresh, local produce. Café DBar in Coolangatta, The Velo Project in Mooloolaba, and Perrotta's at the Gallery in Cairns are popular choices in their respective regions.

3. **Hinterland Retreats:** Queensland's hinterland areas, such as the Scenic Rim and the Sunshine Coast Hinterland, are known for their picturesque landscapes and tranquil settings. These regions are home to charming

cafés and bakeries nestled among rolling hills and lush greenery. You can enjoy locally sourced coffee, homemade pastries, and rustic dishes made with regional ingredients. The Flour Shed in Maleny, The Vintage Apron in Canungra, and Maleny Food Co. are well-regarded establishments in the hinterland.

4. **Artisan Bakeries**: Queensland boasts a number of artisan bakeries that craft a variety of bread, pastries, and cakes using traditional techniques and high-quality ingredients. These bakeries often focus on handcrafted products, from sourdough loaves to delicate croissants and decadent cakes. You can explore bakeries like Flour and Chocolate in Morningside, Jocelyn's Provisions in Fortitude Valley, and Flourish Artisan Bakery in Nambour for an exceptional bakery experience.

5. **Vegan and Specialty Cafés**: Queensland's café scene is also attuned to dietary preferences and special requirements. Vegan and specialty cafés have emerged throughout the state, offering plant-based dishes, gluten-free options, and innovative alternatives to cater to diverse needs. Places like Dicki's in New Farm, Elixiba in Maroochydore, and Sol Bread Bakery in West End provide a range of vegan and specialty treats.

Whether you're in a bustling city, a coastal town, or a serene hinterland setting, Queensland's cafés and bakeries offer a wide selection of coffee, pastries, and baked goods to satisfy your cravings. From cozy neighborhood spots to trendy artisan establishments, these venues provide an inviting atmosphere to relax, socialize, and enjoy the flavors of Queensland.

Vegetarian and Vegan Options

Queensland has embraced the growing demand for vegetarian and vegan options, making it easy for plant-based dinners to find delicious and diverse meals throughout the state. Whether you're looking for dedicated vegan restaurants, vegetarian-friendly eateries, or plant-based twists on traditional cuisine, Queensland offers a range of options to cater to your dietary preferences. Here are some details and information on vegetarian and vegan dining in Queensland:

1. **Brisbane's Plant-Based Scene**: Brisbane, as the capital city of Queensland, is home to a vibrant plant-based dining scene. From fully vegan restaurants to establishments with extensive vegetarian menus, there are numerous options to explore. Venues like Grassfed, Botanica Real Food, and The Green Edge offer a variety of creative and delicious

plant-based dishes, ranging from burgers and pizzas to nourishing bowls and raw desserts.

2. **Vegan Cafés and Juice Bars**: Queensland's cities and coastal regions are teeming with vegan cafés and juice bars that serve up nutritious and flavorful options. These establishments often focus on organic and locally sourced ingredients to create vibrant and wholesome dishes. Places like Nourish Café in Noosa, Flannerys Café in Southport, and Pineapple Express in Brisbane are known for their extensive vegan menus and refreshing juice selections.

3. **Vegetarian-Friendly Ethnic Cuisine**: Queensland's multicultural influence is reflected in its diverse range of vegetarian-friendly ethnic cuisine. Many Indian, Thai, Vietnamese, and Middle Eastern restaurants offer a wide selection of vegetarian and vegan dishes. You can savor

flavorful curries, fragrant rice dishes, fresh spring rolls, and plant-based mezze platters. Venues like Govinda's Vegetarian Restaurant in Brisbane, Happy Boy in Fortitude Valley, and Lonestar Tavern in Mermaid Waters are just a few examples of places that offer vegetarian options within ethnic cuisine.

4. **Health-Focused Restaurants and Retreats**: Queensland's health-conscious culture is evident in the number of restaurants and retreats that prioritize nutritious plant-based meals. These venues often use organic and whole foods to create nourishing dishes that cater to various dietary needs. Retreats such as Gwinganna Lifestyle Retreat in the Gold Coast hinterland and Ebb & Flow in Maroochydore offer plant-based dining experiences, while restaurants like Wild Canary in Brookfield and Blendlove in Nobby Beach specialize in health-focused, vegetarian-friendly cuisine.

5. Vegetarian Festivals and Markets:
Throughout the year, Queensland hosts various vegetarian and vegan festivals, providing an opportunity to explore a wide array of plant-based food options. These events feature food stalls, cooking demonstrations, and live entertainment, celebrating the flavors and benefits of vegetarian and vegan cuisine. The Plant-Based Expo in Brisbane and the Plant-Based Picnic in Maleny are among the popular annual events to discover new vegetarian and vegan treats.

Whether you're a committed vegan or simply looking to incorporate more plant-based meals into your diet, Queensland's vegetarian and vegan dining options are plentiful and diverse. From dedicated vegan eateries to vegetarian-friendly establishments, you'll find a range of delicious and innovative dishes

that highlight the region's fresh produce and
culinary creativity.

Travel Tips and Practical Information

Weather and Climate

Queensland, located in northeastern Australia, is known for its stunning natural landscapes, beautiful beaches, and vibrant cities. When planning a trip to Queensland, it's essential to consider the weather and climate to ensure a comfortable and enjoyable experience. Here are some travel tips and practical information regarding the weather and climate in Queensland:

1. **Climate Zones:**
   - Queensland has a diverse climate due to its size and varying geographical features. The state can be divided into three main climate zones: tropical, subtropical, and temperate.

- The northern region, including popular destinations like Cairns and the Great Barrier Reef, experiences a tropical climate with hot, humid summers and milder, dry winters.

- The southeast coastal region, encompassing cities like Brisbane and the Gold Coast, has a subtropical climate with warm summers, mild winters, and relatively high humidity.

- The inland areas of Queensland have a more temperate climate, characterized by hot summers and cooler winters.

2. **Seasons**:

- Queensland experiences four distinct seasons: summer, autumn, winter, and spring.

- Summer (December to February) is generally hot and humid throughout the state, with temperatures ranging from 25°C to 35°C (77°F to 95°F) in most areas.

- Autumn (March to May) brings milder temperatures, with warm days and cooler evenings. The average temperatures range from 20°C to 30°C (68°F to 86°F).

- Winter (June to August) is the mildest season in most parts of Queensland. Temperatures range from 10°C to 25°C (50°F to 77°F), but can occasionally drop lower in the inland regions.

- Spring (September to November) sees temperatures gradually rising, with average temperatures ranging from 15°C to 30°C (59°F to 86°F).

3. **Rainfall**:

- Queensland's rainfall patterns vary across the state. The coastal regions, especially in the north, experience a wet season during the summer months, with increased chances of tropical storms and cyclones.

- The inland areas and southern regions tend to have a drier climate, with less rainfall throughout the year.

- It's advisable to check the specific rainfall patterns of your chosen destination and pack appropriate clothing and gear accordingly.

4. **UV Index and Sun Protection:**

- Queensland's location close to the equator means that UV radiation levels can be high, even during cooler months. It's important to protect your skin from the sun's harmful rays.

- Apply sunscreen with a high sun protection factor (SPF), wear a hat and sunglasses, and seek shade during the hottest parts of the day.

- Stay hydrated by drinking plenty of water, especially if you're spending time outdoors.

5. **Clothing and Packing:**

- Queensland's climate generally calls for lightweight and breathable clothing due to the warm temperatures. Pack comfortable clothing, including shorts, t-shirts, sundresses, and swimwear.

- Don't forget to bring a light sweater or jacket for cooler evenings or if you plan to visit higher-altitude areas.

- If you're visiting during the wet season, pack a waterproof jacket, umbrella, and suitable footwear.

6. **Check Local Forecasts**:

- Keep an eye on the weather forecasts and updates before and during your trip. This will help you plan your activities accordingly and prepare for any potential weather events.

Remember that Queensland's weather and climate can vary within different regions of the state. It's always a good idea to research the specific weather patterns of your intended destinations and consult reliable sources for the most up-to-date information.

Transportation

When traveling to Queensland, Australia, it's important to familiarize yourself with the transportation options available to make your journey smooth and convenient. Here are some travel tips and practical information regarding transportation in Queensland:

1. **Air Travel**:
   - Queensland has several airports, including major international airports in Brisbane, Cairns, and Gold Coast.
   - Brisbane Airport (BNE) is the state's primary gateway, offering numerous domestic and international flights.
   - Cairns Airport (CNS) serves as a popular entry point for visitors heading to the Great Barrier Reef and tropical North Queensland.
   - Gold Coast Airport (OOL) is convenient for travelers visiting the Gold Coast and southern parts of Queensland.

- Consider booking your flights in advance to secure the best fares and check for any specific travel requirements or restrictions.

2. Domestic Flights:
- If you plan to explore different regions within Queensland, domestic flights are an efficient way to travel long distances quickly.
- Airlines such as Qantas, Virgin Australia, and Jetstar operate frequent domestic flights between major cities and regional centers.
- It's advisable to compare fares and book tickets in advance to secure the best deals.

3. Car Rental:
- Renting a car is a popular option for exploring Queensland, especially if you plan to venture beyond major cities and tourist areas.
- Car rental companies operate in major cities, airports, and regional centers.

- Ensure you have a valid driver's license and consider booking a rental car in advance to guarantee availability.

- Familiarize yourself with Australian road rules, as they may differ from those in your home country.

4. **Public Transportation**:

- Queensland's major cities, including Brisbane, Cairns, and Gold Coast, have reliable public transportation systems.

- Brisbane offers an extensive network of buses, trains, and ferries, operated by TransLink. The go card is a reusable smart card that can be used for fare payment across different modes of transport.

- Cairns has a bus network that connects key areas within the city and nearby attractions.

- Gold Coast has a light rail system (G:link) that runs along the coastline, connecting major tourist destinations.

- Check the schedules and plan your trips accordingly, especially during weekends and public holidays when services may have reduced frequency.

5. **Taxis and Ride-Sharing**:
   - Taxis are readily available in most urban areas of Queensland. You can either hail them on the street or find them at designated taxi ranks.
   - Ride-sharing services like Uber and DiDi operate in major cities, providing an alternative to traditional taxis.
   - Download the relevant apps and set up an account before your trip for ease of use.

6. **Regional Transportation**:
   - If you plan to visit regional areas or islands in Queensland, consider the available transportation options.
   - Ferries and water taxis provide transportation to popular destinations such as

the Great Barrier Reef, Fraser Island, and the Whitsunday Islands.

   - Some remote areas may have limited public transportation options, so it's advisable to research and plan your journey accordingly.

7. **Road Safety and Distances:**

   - If you choose to drive in Queensland, familiarize yourself with the road rules, speed limits, and safety regulations.

   - Queensland has vast distances between attractions, so plan your itinerary with sufficient travel time and rest stops.

   - Take breaks during long drives to combat driver fatigue and stay alert on the roads.

Remember to check the official websites or contact the respective transportation providers for the most up-to-date information on schedules, fares, and any travel restrictions or guidelines that may be in place.

Currency and Banking

When traveling to Queensland, Australia, it's essential to understand the currency and banking system to manage your finances effectively. Here are some travel tips and practical information regarding currency and banking in Queensland:

1. **Currency**:
   - The currency used in Queensland and throughout Australia is the Australian Dollar (AUD).
   - Australian banknotes are available in denominations of $5, $10, $20, $50, and $100. Coins are available in denominations of $2, $1, 50 cents, 20 cents, 10 cents, and 5 cents.
   - It's advisable to familiarize yourself with the appearance of Australian currency to avoid confusion and ensure you receive correct change during transactions.

2. **Exchanging Currency:**

- Currency exchange services are available at major airports, banks, and authorized currency exchange offices in cities and tourist areas.

- It's often more convenient to exchange currency upon arrival at the airport or withdraw local currency from ATMs.

- Compare exchange rates and fees to find the most favorable option, as rates can vary between providers.

3. **ATMs and Cash Withdrawals:**

- ATMs (Automatic Teller Machines) are widely available throughout Queensland in cities, towns, and popular tourist areas.

- Australian ATMs accept major international credit and debit cards such as Visa, Mastercard, American Express, and Maestro.

- Check with your bank or card issuer about any fees or charges for international ATM withdrawals.

- Inform your bank about your travel plans to ensure your card isn't blocked due to suspected fraudulent activity.

4. Credit Cards and Payment Methods:

- Credit cards, such as Visa, Mastercard, and American Express, are widely accepted in most establishments, including hotels, restaurants, shops, and tourist attractions.

- However, it's always a good idea to carry some cash for smaller establishments or places where card payment may not be accepted.

- Contact your credit card company to inquire about any foreign transaction fees or notify them about your travel plans to avoid any potential issues.

5. Banking Hours:

- Banks in Queensland typically operate from Monday to Friday, between 9:30 am and 4:00 pm.

- Some banks may offer extended hours on Thursdays and may have limited or no operations on weekends and public holidays.

- ATMs provide 24/7 access to cash withdrawals and other basic banking services.

6. **Traveler's Cheques**:

- Traveler's cheques are less commonly used nowadays, and it may be challenging to find places that accept them for payment or exchange.

- It's advisable to use other forms of payment, such as cash or cards, for convenience and wider acceptance.

7. **Tipping**:

- Tipping is not as common in Australia as it is in some other countries.

- In restaurants and cafes, it is appreciated to leave a small tip if you are particularly satisfied with the service, but it is not mandatory.

- Tipping for other services, such as taxi rides or hotel staff, is also not expected but can be done for exceptional service.

8. **Online Banking and Mobile Payments:**
   - Online banking and mobile payment apps are widely used in Australia.
   - If you have a local bank account or use digital wallets such as Apple Pay or Google Pay, you can take advantage of these options for convenient and secure transactions.

Remember to inform your bank or credit card company about your travel plans to ensure seamless access to your funds and minimize any potential issues with transactions. Additionally, keep an eye on your belongings and exercise caution when using ATMs or handling cash to protect against theft or fraud.

Health and Safety

When traveling to Queensland, Australia, it's essential to prioritize your health and safety. Here are some travel tips and practical information regarding health and safety in Queensland:

1. **Travel Insurance:**
   - It is highly recommended to have comprehensive travel insurance that covers medical expenses, trip cancellation or interruption, and personal belongings.
   - Ensure that your insurance policy covers any specific activities you plan to undertake, such as adventure sports or scuba diving on the Great Barrier Reef.

2. **Vaccinations and Health Precautions:**
   - Before traveling to Queensland, check if there are any recommended or required vaccinations for your destination. Consult

with a healthcare professional or visit a travel clinic for the latest advice.

- It's important to stay hydrated, especially in the warmer months, by drinking plenty of water and avoiding excessive exposure to the sun.

- Protect yourself from mosquito bites, especially in tropical areas, by using insect repellent and wearing long-sleeved clothing and pants.

3. Emergency Services:

- In case of emergencies, dial 000 for immediate assistance, such as police, ambulance, or fire services.

- If you require non-emergency medical assistance, visit a local hospital or medical clinic. Queensland has a reliable healthcare system, but it's important to have travel insurance to cover any medical expenses.

4. Sun Protection:

- Queensland's sun can be intense, so protect yourself from harmful UV rays by wearing sunscreen with a high sun protection factor (SPF), a wide-brimmed hat, sunglasses, and lightweight clothing that covers your skin.

- Seek shade during the hottest part of the day, typically between 10 am and 4 pm, when the sun's rays are strongest.

5. **Water Safety:**

- Queensland boasts stunning beaches, rivers, and waterways, but it's important to be aware of water safety precautions.

- Only swim at patrolled beaches and follow the instructions of lifeguards.

- Pay attention to warning signs, especially regarding stinger (jellyfish) or crocodile presence in certain areas.

- Familiarize yourself with the local conditions, such as tides and currents, before swimming or participating in water activities.

6. **Wildlife Safety:**

  - Queensland is home to a diverse range of wildlife, including some species that can pose a risk.

  - When exploring natural areas, follow any signage or guidelines provided to ensure your safety and the welfare of the animals.

  - Maintain a safe distance from wildlife, especially if they are wild or potentially dangerous.

  - If you plan to visit the Great Barrier Reef, listen to the safety instructions provided by tour operators regarding snorkeling or diving near marine creatures.

7. **General Safety:**

  - Queensland is a relatively safe destination, but it's always important to exercise common sense and take basic safety precautions.

  - Be mindful of your personal belongings and avoid displaying valuable items in public.

- Stay informed about current safety conditions, such as weather warnings or any potential hazards in the area you plan to visit.

It's advisable to stay updated on the latest travel advisories and guidelines from relevant authorities before and during your trip to Queensland. Additionally, consult with your healthcare provider or visit travel health websites for any specific health recommendations or precautions based on your individual circumstances.

Language and Communication

When traveling to Queensland, Australia, understanding the language and communication options can greatly enhance your experience. Here are some travel tips and practical information regarding language and communication in Queensland:

1. **Official Language:**

   - The official language of Australia is English, and this includes Queensland. English is widely spoken and understood throughout the state.

   - You can communicate with locals, hotel staff, and service providers in English without any significant language barriers.

2. **Local Slang and Expressions:**

   - Like many regions, Queensland has its own unique slang and expressions. Some common phrases you may come across include:

- "G'day" - a common greeting, short for "good day"
- "No worries" - an expression meaning "it's okay" or "you're welcome"
- "Mate" - a term often used to address someone casually, similar to "buddy" or "friend"
- "Arvo" - short for "afternoon"
- Don't be afraid to ask locals for clarification or explanations if you come across unfamiliar slang terms.

3. Multilingual Services:

- In popular tourist areas, such as Brisbane and the Gold Coast, you may encounter multilingual staff in hotels, tourist information centers, and major attractions.
- While English is the predominant language, you may find individuals who can communicate in other languages, such as Mandarin, Japanese, or German.

- However, it's always a good idea to have a basic understanding of English to ensure smooth communication and navigate day-to-day interactions.

4. **Mobile Phone Coverage**:
   - Queensland has excellent mobile phone coverage across most areas, including cities, towns, and major tourist destinations.
   - Check with your mobile service provider to ensure that your phone plan includes coverage in Australia. Consider activating international roaming or purchasing a local SIM card for cost-effective local communication.
   - Free Wi-Fi is often available in hotels, cafes, and public spaces, allowing you to stay connected and use internet-based communication apps.

5. **Emergency Services:**
   - In case of emergencies, dial 000 for immediate assistance. This number can be

used to contact the police, ambulance, or fire services.

  - Queensland emergency services operators are trained to handle calls in English and can provide assistance in various situations.

6. **Translation Apps and Phrasebooks**:

  - If you're not fluent in English, consider using translation apps or carrying a pocket-sized phrasebook to help with basic communication.

  - Popular translation apps such as Google Translate or iTranslate can help you translate words, phrases, or even have real-time conversations.

7. **Cultural Sensitivity**:

  - While English is widely spoken, it's important to be mindful of cultural sensitivity and respect local customs and traditions.

  - Be patient and understanding when communicating with individuals who may have limited English proficiency, and make an effort to bridge any language barriers with gestures and a friendly demeanor.

Remember, Queensland is a welcoming destination where English is the primary language of communication. By being prepared and open-minded, you can navigate the language and communicate effectively to make the most of your travel experience.

Customs and Etiquette

When visiting Queensland, Australia, it's important to familiarize yourself with the local customs and etiquette to ensure a respectful and enjoyable experience. Here are some travel tips and practical information regarding customs and etiquette in Queensland:

1. **Greetings and Politeness:**
   - Australians generally greet each other with a casual "G'day" or a simple "Hello." Handshakes are common when meeting someone for the first time.
   - Queenslanders are known for their friendly and laid-back nature, so maintaining a polite and respectful demeanor is appreciated.

2. **Punctuality:**
   - Queenslanders value punctuality, so it's considered courteous to arrive on time for scheduled appointments, meetings, or tours.

- If you're running late, it's polite to inform the person or organization you're meeting as soon as possible.

3. Queuing and Waiting in Line:

- Australians are generally respectful of queues and waiting in line. Make sure to join the end of a line and wait patiently for your turn.

- Cutting in line or attempting to jump ahead is considered impolite and may be met with disapproval.

4. Personal Space and Respect:

- Queenslanders appreciate personal space and respecting the personal boundaries of others. Avoid standing too close to people unless necessary.

- When conversing, maintain a comfortable distance and avoid touching or hugging someone you have just met unless they initiate it.

5. **Tipping and Service Charges:**

   - Tipping is not a common practice in Australia, including Queensland, as service charges are usually included in the bill.

   - If you receive exceptional service or would like to show appreciation, a small tip is welcomed but not expected.

6. **Environmental Awareness:**

   - Queensland is renowned for its natural beauty and pristine environments. It's important to practice responsible tourism and respect the environment.

   - Dispose of rubbish in designated bins, follow any signage or guidelines regarding wildlife protection, and refrain from littering or damaging natural areas.

7. **Alcohol Consumption and Smoking:**

   - Drinking alcohol in public places is generally restricted in Queensland. It is advisable to consume alcoholic beverages in licensed venues such as bars, restaurants, or designated outdoor areas.

- Smoking is prohibited in many public spaces, including restaurants, bars, and public transport. Look for designated smoking areas if you need to smoke.

8. Aboriginal and Torres Strait Islander Culture:

- Queensland has a rich Indigenous heritage, and it's important to show respect for Aboriginal and Torres Strait Islander cultures.

- When visiting Indigenous sites, follow any guidelines provided, show reverence, and refrain from touching or removing any cultural or historical artifacts.

- Seek permission before taking photographs of Indigenous people, and always ask for consent if you wish to learn or participate in cultural activities.

9. Sun Safety:

   - Queensland has a sunny climate, and sun safety is crucial. Protect yourself from harmful UV rays by wearing sunscreen, hats, and sunglasses, and seeking shade during the hottest part of the day.

10. Dress Code:

   - Queensland has a relaxed and casual dress code. Lightweight and comfortable clothing is suitable for most occasions.

   - However, some upscale restaurants, theaters, or events may have a dress code, so it's advisable to check beforehand.

By respecting local customs and practicing good etiquette, you can foster positive interactions with locals and create memorable experiences during your visit to Queensland. Remember to embrace the friendly and laid-back atmosphere that the state is known for and enjoy your time exploring its natural wonders and vibrant cities.

Festivals and Events

Queensland, Australia, is known for its vibrant festivals and events throughout the year. Here are some travel tips and practical information regarding festivals and events in Queensland:

1. **Major Festivals and Events**:
   - Brisbane Festival: Held annually in September, the Brisbane Festival is a multi-disciplinary arts festival featuring music, dance, theater, and visual arts performances.
   - Woodford Folk Festival: Taking place from late December to early January in Woodfordia, this renowned festival showcases music, art, workshops, and cultural experiences.
   - Cairns Indigenous Art Fair: Held in July in Cairns, this event celebrates the arts and culture of Aboriginal and Torres Strait Islander communities through exhibitions, performances, and workshops.

- Caloundra Music Festival: Held in October, this popular music festival takes place in Caloundra and features a diverse lineup of Australian and international artists.

2. **Local Celebrations and Events:**
- Ekka: The Royal Queensland Show, commonly known as Ekka, is an iconic agricultural show held in Brisbane in August. It offers a range of entertainment, exhibitions, and activities, including animal shows, live music, and show rides.
- Noosa Food and Wine Festival: This annual festival in Noosa showcases the region's food and wine culture with cooking demonstrations, tastings, and celebrity chef appearances.
- Airlie Beach Festival of Music: Held in November, this music festival in Airlie Beach features performances by national and international artists across multiple venues.

- Opera at Jimbour: Set in the picturesque Jimbour House, this open-air opera event held in July presents a spectacular showcase of opera and classical music.

3. **Planning and Tickets:**

- Check the official websites or local tourism websites for the most up-to-date information on festivals and events in Queensland.

- Purchase tickets in advance for popular events to secure your spot, as some events may sell out quickly.

- Consider accommodation options well in advance, as festivals and events often attract large crowds and may affect availability.

4. **Weather Considerations**:

- Queensland's festivals and events can take place throughout the year, so be mindful of the weather conditions during your visit.

- Pack appropriate clothing and accessories such as sunscreen, hats, and umbrellas based on the season and expected weather.

5. Local Customs and Etiquette:

- Respect the rules and regulations of each event, including any restrictions on food, drinks, or photography.
- Embrace the festive atmosphere and engage with locals, artists, and performers to enhance your experience.
- Be aware of the noise levels and be considerate of the local community if attending events held in residential areas.

6. Transportation and Parking:

- Festivals and events can attract significant crowds, so plan your transportation in advance.
- Public transportation, such as trains, buses, or ferries, may offer special services

during major events. Check the schedules and routes in advance.

 - If driving, be prepared for increased traffic and limited parking options near event venues. Consider carpooling or utilizing designated event parking areas.

7. Accessibility:

 - Many festivals and events in Queensland strive to provide accessibility for all attendees. Check event websites for information on wheelchair access, companion tickets, and other accommodations.

8. Local Cuisine and Food Vendors:

 - Festivals and events often offer a variety of food vendors showcasing local cuisine and international flavors. Take the opportunity to sample different dishes and explore the culinary offerings.

Remember to stay updated with event details, including any changes or cancellations, by checking official websites and local sources closer to the date of your visit. Enjoy the vibrant atmosphere, immerse yourself in the local culture, and make the most of your festival or event experience in Queensland.

Itineraries

One Week in Queensland

One Week Itinerary in Queensland, Australia

Day 1: Arrival in Brisbane and City Exploration

- Arrive at Brisbane Airport and transfer to your accommodation in the city.
- Start your exploration of Brisbane, Queensland's capital city. Visit popular attractions such as South Bank Parklands, Brisbane Botanic Gardens, and the Queensland Museum.
- Take a leisurely walk along the Brisbane River and enjoy the vibrant atmosphere of the city.
- In the evening, explore the trendy dining and entertainment precincts of Fortitude Valley or James Street.

183

Day 2: Fraser Island Adventure

- Depart from Brisbane early in the morning for a full-day trip to Fraser Island, the largest sand island in the world.
- Explore the island's unique landscapes, including pristine beaches, crystal-clear lakes, and dense rainforests.
- Take a guided 4WD tour or join a scenic flight over the island for breathtaking views.
- Swim in the famous Lake McKenzie and enjoy a picnic lunch in the wilderness.
- Return to Brisbane in the evening and relax at your accommodation.

Day 3: Great Barrier Reef Experience

- Fly from Brisbane to Cairns, the gateway to the Great Barrier Reef.
- Embark on a full-day reef tour, where you can snorkel or scuba dive among vibrant coral reefs, encountering an array of marine life.

- Enjoy a delicious buffet lunch on board the tour vessel while surrounded by the stunning reef.
- Take part in additional activities like underwater photography, semi-submersible rides, or a scenic helicopter flight over the reef.
- Return to Cairns in the late afternoon and explore the night markets or relax at your hotel.

Day 4: Cairns and Daintree Rainforest
- Venture north from Cairns to explore the ancient Daintree Rainforest, a UNESCO World Heritage Site.
- Take a guided tour through the lush rainforest, learning about its unique flora and fauna.
- Visit Mossman Gorge and take a refreshing swim in the clear waters of the Mossman River.

- Discover the Daintree River on a wildlife cruise, spotting crocodiles, exotic birds, and other wildlife.
- Return to Cairns and enjoy dinner at one of the waterfront restaurants.

Day 5: Whitsunday Islands Paradise
- Fly from Cairns to the Whitsunday Coast and transfer to Airlie Beach.
- Join a full-day sailing trip to explore the stunning Whitsunday Islands, famous for their white sandy beaches and turquoise waters.
- Snorkel in the Great Barrier Reef Marine Park, relax on pristine beaches, and indulge in a gourmet picnic lunch.
- If time allows, take a scenic hike to Hill Inlet to witness the breathtaking swirling sands of Whitehaven Beach.
- Return to Airlie Beach and unwind at your hotel or explore the vibrant town's nightlife.

Day 6: Gold Coast Adventure

- Fly from the Whitsunday Coast to the Gold Coast, known for its beautiful beaches and thrilling theme parks.
- Spend the day enjoying the rides and attractions at one of the theme parks like Dreamworld, Movie World, or Sea World.
- Alternatively, relax on the famous Surfers Paradise Beach or explore the shopping and dining options along Cavill Avenue.
- In the evening, take a leisurely stroll along the beachfront and enjoy dinner at one of the coastal restaurants.

Day 7: Gold Coast Hinterland and Departure

- Explore the scenic Gold Coast Hinterland, just a short drive from the coast.
- Visit the charming mountain villages of Tamborine Mountain or Springbrook and discover their lush rainforests, waterfalls, and panoramic lookouts.

- Enjoy a leisurely hike or explore the area's art galleries, boutique wineries, and local markets.

Two-Week Itinerary in Queensland, Australia

Day 1-3: Brisbane City Exploration and Surrounds

- Arrive in Brisbane and spend the first few days exploring the city and its surrounding areas.
- Visit popular attractions such as South Bank Parklands, the Queensland Museum, and Brisbane Botanic Gardens.
- Take a day trip to Moreton Island and enjoy activities like snorkeling, sandboarding, and exploring the Tangalooma Wrecks.
- Explore the nearby Sunshine Coast, visiting Noosa Heads, Australia Zoo, and the stunning Glass House Mountains.

Day 4-6: Fraser Island Adventure and Hervey Bay

- Depart from Brisbane and embark on a multi-day tour to Fraser Island, the largest sand island in the world.
- Explore the island's unique landscapes, including Lake McKenzie, Eli Creek, and the Maheno Shipwreck.
- Take part in 4WD tours, bushwalks, and swimming in the island's pristine lakes and creeks.
- After Fraser Island, head to Hervey Bay, known as the gateway to the famous whale-watching destination.
- Take a whale-watching cruise and spot humpback whales during their annual migration (seasonal availability).

Day 7-9: Cairns and the Great Barrier Reef
- Fly from Hervey Bay to Cairns, the gateway to the Great Barrier Reef.
- Spend a few days exploring Cairns and its surrounding areas.

- Join a full-day reef tour to snorkel or scuba dive among the vibrant coral reefs of the Great Barrier Reef.
- Visit the Daintree Rainforest, a UNESCO World Heritage Site, and take a guided tour through its ancient landscapes.
- Explore the vibrant nightlife and dining scene in Cairns and enjoy the city's tropical ambiance.

Day 10-12: Whitsunday Islands and Airlie Beach
- Fly from Cairns to the Whitsunday Coast and transfer to Airlie Beach.
- Join a multi-day sailing trip to explore the stunning Whitsunday Islands.
- Snorkel in the Great Barrier Reef Marine Park, relax on pristine beaches, and witness the swirling sands of Whitehaven Beach.
- Enjoy water activities like kayaking, paddleboarding, and fishing.

- Take a scenic hike in the Whitsunday Islands National Park for breathtaking views.
- Indulge in the local cuisine and vibrant nightlife of Airlie Beach.

Day 13-14: Gold Coast and Hinterland
- Fly from the Whitsunday Coast to the Gold Coast, known for its beautiful beaches and thrilling theme parks.
- Spend a day enjoying the rides and attractions at one of the theme parks like Dreamworld, Movie World, or Sea World.
- Explore the Gold Coast Hinterland, visiting Tamborine Mountain, Springbrook, and Lamington National Park.
- Discover lush rainforests, stunning waterfalls, and take in panoramic views from various lookouts.
- Relax on the famous Surfers Paradise Beach and explore the vibrant dining and shopping scene.

- On the final day, take in any remaining activities or attractions before departing from the Gold Coast.

This two-week itinerary provides a well-rounded experience of Queensland, covering city exploration, island adventures, rainforest exploration, and coastal relaxation. Remember to check seasonal availability and book in advance for tours and accommodations.

Family-Friendly Adventures

Family-Friendly Adventures in Queensland, Australia

Day 1: Arrival in Brisbane and City Exploration

- Arrive at Brisbane Airport and transfer to your family-friendly accommodation in the city.
- Explore South Bank Parklands, a vibrant waterfront precinct with playgrounds, a man-made beach, and the Wheel of Brisbane.
- Visit the Queensland Museum and Sciencentre, offering interactive exhibits and educational activities for children.
- Enjoy a relaxing walk along the Brisbane River and have dinner at a family-friendly restaurant.

Day 2: Australia Zoo and Sunshine Coast

- Take a day trip to Australia Zoo, located on the Sunshine Coast. This famous zoo was founded by the late Steve Irwin and offers a variety of animal encounters and shows.

- Get up close with kangaroos, koalas, crocodiles, and other Australian wildlife.
- Afterward, visit the nearby Sunshine Coast and spend the rest of the day exploring Noosa Heads, where you can relax on the beach or take a nature walk in Noosa National Park.

Day 3: Moreton Island Adventure

- Embark on a family-friendly adventure to Moreton Island, accessible by a short ferry ride from Brisbane.
- Enjoy snorkeling around the Tangalooma Wrecks, where colorful marine life can be seen.
- Experience sandboarding on the island's massive sand dunes or take a quad bike tour.
- Relax and swim in the crystal-clear waters of the island's beaches.
- End the day with a sunset dolphin feeding experience at Tangalooma Island Resort.

Day 4-6: Gold Coast Theme Parks and Surfers Paradise
- Travel to the Gold Coast, known for its thrilling theme parks and family-friendly attractions.
- Spend a day at Dreamworld, where you can enjoy roller coasters, water slides, and interactive animal encounters.
- Visit Warner Bros. Movie World to experience movie-themed rides and meet your favorite characters.
- Explore Sea World, offering marine animal shows, rides, and educational exhibits.
- Spend time on the famous Surfers Paradise Beach, where you can swim, build sandcastles, and enjoy beachside activities.

Day 7-9: Cairns and Great Barrier Reef
- Fly from the Gold Coast to Cairns, a family-friendly destination offering access to the Great Barrier Reef and rainforests.

- Take a cruise to the Great Barrier Reef, where the whole family can enjoy snorkeling or take a semi-submersible tour to observe the underwater world.
- Visit the Cairns Zoom and Wildlife Dome, a unique wildlife experience located in the heart of the city.
- Explore the Cairns Esplanade, featuring a large lagoon pool, playgrounds, and barbecue areas.
- Take a day trip to Kuranda, where you can ride the Scenic Railway, visit the Koala Gardens, and explore the rainforest.

Day 10-12: Whitsunday Islands and Airlie Beach

- Fly from Cairns to the Whitsunday Coast and transfer to family-friendly accommodation in Airlie Beach.
- Join a family-friendly sailing trip to explore the beautiful Whitsunday Islands.

- Spend time at Whitehaven Beach, known for its pure white silica sand and crystal-clear waters.
- Enjoy family water activities like snorkeling, paddleboarding, and swimming in secluded bays.
- Take a guided bushwalk in the Whitsunday Islands National Park to discover unique flora and fauna.

Day 13: Cairns Aquarium and Cairns Botanic Gardens
- Return to Cairns and visit the Cairns Aquarium, offering an immersive experience of the region's marine life.
- Explore interactive displays, touch tanks, and educational exhibits suitable for all ages.
- Spend the afternoon at the Cairns Botanic Gardens, where you can picnic, stroll through the gardens.

Romantic Getaways

Romantic Getaways in Queensland, Australia

Day 1: Arrival in Brisbane and Romantic Dinner
- Arrive at Brisbane Airport and transfer to your romantic accommodation in the city.
- Enjoy a leisurely stroll along the Brisbane River and take in the beautiful views.
- Indulge in a romantic dinner at one of the fine dining restaurants overlooking the river.
- Take a moonlit walk through the city and enjoy the vibrant nightlife.

Day 2: Scenic Drive to the Sunshine Coast
- Rent a car and embark on a scenic drive to the Sunshine Coast, a picturesque coastal region.
- Visit the charming town of Montville in the Sunshine Coast Hinterland, known for its stunning views and boutique shops.

- Enjoy a romantic lunch at a local café and explore the art galleries and craft shops.
- In the afternoon, head to the beautiful coastal town of Noosa Heads and relax on the beach or take a romantic walk in Noosa National Park.

Day 3: Relaxation and Pampering in the Gold Coast
- Fly or drive from the Sunshine Coast to the Gold Coast, a renowned destination for luxury and relaxation.
- Check into a luxurious resort or spa hotel and indulge in a day of pampering treatments.
- Spend the afternoon lounging by the pool or on the beach, enjoying the sun and each other's company.
- In the evening, have a romantic dinner at a waterfront restaurant and take a moonlit stroll along the beach.

Day 4-6: Whitsunday Islands Paradise

- Fly from the Gold Coast to the Whitsunday Coast and transfer to a secluded resort or private villa in the Whitsunday Islands.
- Enjoy days of pure relaxation and romance in this tropical paradise.
- Take a romantic sailing trip to explore the pristine beaches and turquoise waters of the Whitsunday Islands.
- Indulge in couples' spa treatments, private beach picnics, and sunset cruises.
- Spend time at the famous Whitehaven Beach, known for its stunning beauty and seclusion.

Day 7-9: Port Douglas and the Great Barrier Reef
- Fly from the Whitsunday Coast to Cairns and transfer to Port Douglas, a charming coastal town.
- Stay at a luxurious resort or boutique hotel in Port Douglas and enjoy the relaxed tropical atmosphere.

- Take a romantic cruise to the Great Barrier Reef and snorkel or scuba dive among the colorful coral reefs.
- Explore the Daintree Rainforest, a UNESCO World Heritage Site, on a guided tour.
- Enjoy romantic dinners at waterfront restaurants and take evening strolls along Four Mile Beach.

Day 10-12: Romantic Rainforest Retreat in the Atherton Tablelands
- Drive from Port Douglas to the Atherton Tablelands, a region known for its lush rainforests and waterfalls.
- Stay at a secluded rainforest retreat or eco-lodge and immerse yourselves in nature.
- Take romantic walks through the rainforest, visit picturesque waterfalls, and swim in natural pools.
- Enjoy intimate candlelit dinners at your accommodation or dine at a gourmet restaurant in the area.

- Visit local wineries and indulge in wine tasting experiences.

Day 13: Relaxation and Farewell in Brisbane
- Drive or fly back to Brisbane for your final day of relaxation and farewell.
- Check into a luxury hotel in the city and enjoy the amenities, such as rooftop pools or spa facilities.
- Spend the day shopping at boutique stores, exploring art galleries, or simply enjoying each other's company.
- In the evening, have a romantic farewell dinner at a top-rated restaurant in Brisbane.

Day 14: Departure
- Depart from Brisbane, cherishing the memories of your romantic getaway in Queensland.

Adventure Seekers' Guide in Queensland, Australia

Day 1: Arrive in Cairns and Rainforest Ziplining

- Arrive at Cairns Airport and transfer to your accommodation in the city.
- Start your adventure by experiencing the thrill of ziplining through the lush rainforest canopy.
- Join a guided ziplining tour in the Cairns region, such as in the Daintree Rainforest or in the nearby Atherton Tablelands.
- Enjoy the adrenaline rush as you soar through the treetops, taking in breathtaking views of the surrounding landscapes.
- Return to Cairns and explore the vibrant nightlife and dining options.

Day 2: Scuba Diving in the Great Barrier Reef

- Embark on an unforgettable scuba diving adventure in the Great Barrier Reef, a UNESCO World Heritage Site.
- Join a diving tour from Cairns or Port Douglas and explore the diverse marine ecosystem.
- Dive into the crystal-clear waters, encountering colorful coral reefs, tropical fish, and other marine creatures.
- Certified divers can enjoy exploring deeper dive sites, while beginners can try an introductory dive under the guidance of experienced instructors.
- After the dive, relax on the tour vessel and soak in the beauty of the reef.

Day 3: Skydiving in Airlie Beach
- Fly from Cairns to Airlie Beach, a coastal town known for its thrilling adventure activities.

- Experience the ultimate adrenaline rush by skydiving over the stunning Whitsunday Islands.
- Take a tandem skydive with an experienced instructor, freefalling from high above and enjoying breathtaking views of the islands and the Great Barrier Reef.
- After landing, celebrate your skydiving achievement and spend the rest of the day relaxing on the beach or exploring Airlie Beach.

Day 4-6: Outdoor Adventure in the Gold Coast
- Fly from the Whitsunday Coast to the Gold Coast, a paradise for adventure seekers.
- Spend a few days indulging in a variety of outdoor activities.
- Go surfing at some of Australia's best surf beaches, such as Burleigh Heads or Snapper Rocks.

- Try your hand at jet skiing, wakeboarding, or parasailing in the calm waters of the Broadwater.
- Take a thrilling jet boat ride along the Gold Coast's waterways, experiencing high-speed maneuvers and 360-degree spins.
- For an aerial adventure, go sky-high with a tandem parasailing experience, enjoying panoramic views of the coastline.
- End your days with a relaxing stroll along the beach or enjoy the vibrant nightlife in Surfers Paradise.

Day 7-9: Hiking and Rock Climbing in the Sunshine Coast
- Travel from the Gold Coast to the Sunshine Coast, a region offering a diverse range of adventure activities.
- Explore the stunning Glass House Mountains and embark on a hiking adventure.
- Climb one of the peaks, such as Mount Ngungun or Mount Tibrogargan, for

panoramic views of the surrounding landscapes.

- Join a rock climbing tour in the Sunshine Coast Hinterland, scaling the cliffs and challenging yourself with different routes.
- Discover the natural beauty of the region as you conquer the heights.
- Spend time exploring the coastal towns of Noosa Heads and Mooloolaba, where you can try stand-up paddleboarding, kayaking, or even take a surfing lesson.

Day 10-12: Fraser Island 4WD Adventure
- Depart from the Sunshine Coast and head to Fraser Island, the largest sand island in the world.
- Embark on an exhilarating 4WD adventure across the island, exploring its unique landscapes.
- Drive along the beach highways and navigate through challenging sand tracks.

- Discover the stunning beauty of the island, including Lake McKenzie, Eli Creek, and the Maheno Shipwreck.

Additional Resources

Useful Websites and Apps

**1. Queensland Government Website
(www.qld.gov.au):** The official website of the
Queensland Government provides a wealth of
information and resources for residents and
visitors. It covers various aspects such as
education, health, transport, business,
tourism, and more.

2. TransLink (www.translink.com.au):
TransLink is the official public transport
website for Queensland. It offers information
on bus, train, and ferry services, including
timetables, fares, and journey planning tools.
The website also provides real-time updates
on service disruptions and alerts.

**3. Queensland National Parks
(www.npsr.qld.gov.au):** This website is

managed by the Queensland Department of Environment and Science and offers comprehensive information about the national parks in Queensland. It provides details on park locations, facilities, camping, hiking trails, and wildlife encounters.

4. **MyPolice Queensland (www.mypolice.qld.gov.au)**: MyPolice is an online platform that allows Queensland residents to connect with their local police. It provides access to news, community alerts, crime statistics, and the ability to report non-urgent incidents and provide information anonymously.

5. **Queensland Health (www.health.qld.gov.au)**: The Queensland Health website offers a range of health-related information and services. It provides updates on public health alerts, information on hospitals and healthcare

facilities, resources for specific health conditions, and access to online services such as appointment booking and health records.

6. Queensland Museum (www.qm.qld.gov.au): The Queensland Museum website is a valuable resource for those interested in the state's natural and cultural history. It features virtual exhibitions, educational resources, research publications, and information on upcoming events and programs.

7. Bureau of Meteorology (www.bom.gov.au/qld): The Bureau of Meteorology's Queensland section provides weather forecasts, warnings, and observations for the state. It includes detailed information on current conditions, radar and satellite imagery, climate data, and severe weather updates.

8. RACQ Road Conditions
(www.racq.com.au/travel/Maps-and-Road-C
onditions/Road-Conditions): RACQ (Royal
Automobile Club of Queensland) offers a road
conditions website that provides up-to-date
information on road closures, traffic
congestion, and hazards across Queensland. It
is a valuable resource for planning travel
routes and ensuring road safety.

9. QAGOMA (www.qagoma.qld.gov.au): The
Queensland Art Gallery and Gallery of Modern
Art (QAGOMA) website is an excellent
resource for art enthusiasts. It features
information on current and upcoming
exhibitions, artist profiles, educational
programs, and online collections.

10. BookitNow (www.bookitnow.qld.gov.au):
BookitNow is a Queensland government
website that allows users to make online
bookings for various recreational activities,

including camping, tours, and events. It provides a convenient platform for planning and booking outdoor adventures across the state.

11. **Queensland Libraries (www.libraries.qld.gov.au):** The Queensland Libraries website provides access to the vast collection of resources and services offered by public libraries across the state. Users can search for books, e-books, audiobooks, and other media, as well as access online databases, educational resources, and community programs.

12. **QLDTraffic (qldtraffic.qld.gov.au):** QLDTraffic is a website and app that offers real-time traffic information, road closures, and travel times in Queensland. It helps commuters and travelers plan their journeys efficiently and avoid congestion.

These resources and websites provide valuable information and services to residents, visitors, and tourists in Queensland. Whether you are looking for government services, transportation options, outdoor activities, cultural experiences, health information, or simply staying updated with local news.

Recommended Reading

1. **"The Secret River" by Kate Grenville**: This historical novel explores the early settlement of Queensland and the conflicts between the Indigenous Australians and European settlers. It offers a thought-provoking insight into the impact of colonization on the region.

2. **"Conspiracy of Silence**: Queensland's Frontier Killing Times" by Timothy Bottoms: This book delves into the dark history of Queensland's frontier violence during the 19th century. It uncovers the truth about massacres and the dispossession of Indigenous peoples, shedding light on an often overlooked aspect of Australian history.

3. **"Island Home:** A Landscape Memoir" by Tim Winton: Although not specifically focused on Queensland, this memoir by renowned Australian author Tim Winton captures the essence of the Australian landscape, including

the coastal regions of Queensland. It reflects on the author's deep connection to the natural environment and its impact on his identity.

4. "**Queensland**: Everything You Ever Wanted to Know But Were Afraid to Ask" by Colin Hooper: This comprehensive guidebook provides an in-depth exploration of Queensland's history, geography, culture, and attractions. It covers everything from the Great Barrier Reef and the Daintree Rainforest to the Outback and iconic cities like Brisbane and Cairns.

5. "**The Great Barrier Reef**: A Journey Through the World's Greatest Natural Wonder" by Len Zell: This visually stunning book takes readers on a journey through the spectacular ecosystems of the Great Barrier Reef. It showcases the diversity of marine life, coral reefs, and the conservation challenges faced by this UNESCO World Heritage site.

6. **"Queensland:** A Biography" by Ross Fitzgerald and John Cribbin: This engaging biography provides an overview of Queensland's evolution from its early colonial days to the present. It explores the state's political history, social changes, economic development, and the unique character that sets Queensland apart from other Australian states.

7. **"A Short History of Queensland" by Raymond Evans**: For those seeking a concise overview of Queensland's history, this book offers a valuable resource. It covers key events, significant figures, and the state's transformation over time, from its Indigenous origins to modern-day Queensland.

8. **"The Daintree Blockade:** The Battle for Australia's Tropical Rainforests" by Bill Wilkie: This book recounts the environmental

activism and protests that led to the protection of the Daintree Rainforest in Far North Queensland. It explores the challenges faced by conservationists and the importance of preserving this ancient ecosystem.

9. **"Queensland's Outback:** A Visitor's Guide" by Mike Kersh: This travel guide is perfect for those planning to explore Queensland's vast Outback region. It provides detailed information on attractions, road trips, camping, wildlife encounters, and the unique landscapes that define this remote and rugged part of the state.

10. **"Queensland's Best Bush, Coast & City Walks" by Dianne McLay:** This guidebook features a collection of scenic walks and hikes across Queensland. It includes trails through rainforests, coastal tracks, mountain treks, and urban walks, offering options for all

fitness levels and showcasing the state's natural beauty.

These recommended reading materials provide valuable insights into the history, culture, environment, and diverse landscapes of Queensland. Whether you're interested in Queensland's past, its natural wonders, or planning a visit to the state, these books offer a deeper understanding and appreciation for all that Queensland has to offer.

Maps and Guides

1. **Queensland Maps** - Queensland Government (www.qld.gov.au/maps): The official website of the Queensland Government offers a variety of maps for different purposes. These maps cover areas such as road networks, national parks, coastal regions, and local government boundaries. They are useful for planning trips, exploring outdoor activities, and understanding the geography of Queensland.

2. **Explore Queensland Map** - Tourism and Events Queensland (www.queensland.com/map): The Explore Queensland Map provided by Tourism and Events Queensland is an interactive online tool that allows users to explore different regions of the state. It highlights popular destinations, attractions, accommodation options, and suggested itineraries. The map is

a helpful resource for planning vacations and discovering the best of Queensland.

3. **Queensland Road Map** - RACQ (Royal Automobile Club of Queensland) (www.racq.com.au/travel/Maps-and-Road-Conditions/Road-Maps): RACQ offers detailed road maps of Queensland, including major highways, regional roads, and towns. These maps provide information on distances, travel times, rest areas, and fuel stations. They are essential for road trips and navigating the state's road network.

4. **Queensland Camping Guide** - Queensland Government (www.qld.gov.au/recreation/activities/camping): The Queensland Camping Guide is a comprehensive resource for camping enthusiasts. It provides information on campsites, facilities, booking procedures, and camping regulations in national parks, state

forests, and other designated camping areas. The guide helps outdoor enthusiasts plan camping trips and enjoy Queensland's natural beauty.

5. Queensland National Parks and Forests Guide - Queensland National Parks (www.npsr.qld.gov.au/parks): The Queensland National Parks and Forests Guide offers detailed information on the state's national parks, including maps, walking trails, camping sites, and visitor facilities. It also highlights the unique flora, fauna, and geological features found in each park. The guide is a valuable tool for nature lovers and adventure seekers.

6. **Queensland Coastal Access Maps** - Queensland Government (www.qld.gov.au/recreation/activities/beach-surf): The Queensland Coastal Access Maps provide information on beach access points,

surf lifesaving clubs, and designated swimming areas along the coast. They also highlight coastal walking and cycling tracks, picnic spots, and other recreational activities. These maps are useful for beachgoers and those looking to explore Queensland's stunning coastline.

7. **Queensland Heritage Trails Guide** - Queensland Government (www.qld.gov.au/recreation/heritage/trails): The Queensland Heritage Trails Guide showcases the state's rich heritage and historical sites. It features self-guided walking and driving trails that take visitors through important cultural and historical landmarks, including heritage-listed buildings, archaeological sites, and Indigenous cultural sites. The guide offers a fascinating glimpse into Queensland's past.

8. **Queensland Wine and Food Trail Maps** - Queensland Government (www.qld.gov.au/recreation/food/homegrown/food-trails): For food and wine enthusiasts, the Queensland Wine and Food Trail Maps provide information on the state's top food and wine regions. These maps highlight cellar doors, farm gates, farmers' markets, and gourmet trails where visitors can sample local produce and culinary delights. They are a great resource for gastronomic adventures in Queensland.

9. **Queensland Bird Trails Guide** - BirdLife Australia (www.birdlife.org.au/visit-us/qld-bird-trails): The Queensland Bird Trails Guide is designed for birdwatchers and nature enthusiasts. It offers maps and information on bird watching locations, bird species, and important bird areas across Queensland. The guide helps

birdwatchers explore diverse habitats and spot a wide range of bird species in the state.

10. **Queensland Travel Guides** - Lonely Planet (www.lonelyplanet.com/australia/queensland).

Made in the USA
Monee, IL
03 January 2025

76006392R00125

ISBN 9798856889818

9 798856 889818

900